The Foreclosure Workbook:

The Complete Guide to Understanding Foreclosure and Saving Your Home

Carla Douglin

xulon PRESS

The Foreclosure Workbook:
The Complete Guide to Understanding Foreclosure and Saving Your Home
by Carla Douglin

Printed in the United States of America

ISBN 978-1-60266-968-0

Publisher's Note:
The Information contained within this publication has been condensed from the well-known delinquency and foreclosure practices of the FNMA, HUD, the Veterans Administration and other providers of real-estate mortgages both public and private. The practice and procedures outlined here apply universally to loan administration policies throughout the mortgage industry. Certain policies and practice attributed here to Fannie Mae do not reflect the current policy of all lenders, or the manner in which an such policy may be applied, or effect the outcome of a borrower's particular situation.

Legal Disclaimer:
Dominion Foreclosure Consulting Services, Inc. is not a law firm. We do not provide legal advice. These guidelines are not to be construed as legal advice or the practicing of law.

This product and any related services or content are designed to operate and provide information with the understanding that Dominion Foreclosure Consulting Services, Inc. and its representatives are not engaged in rendering legal, accounting, or other professional service. If legal advice or other expert assistance is required, the service of a competent professional should be sought. Dominion Foreclosure will satisfy any statutory or regulatory obligations, or will assist with, guarantee or otherwise ensure compliance with, any applicable laws or regulations. You are solely responsible for ensuring that your use of this book, related services or content is in accordance with applicable law. It is your responsibility to keep abreast of changes in laws, regulations and accounting practices that affect you and your finances.

www.xulonpress.com

Dedication

This book is dedicated to my family:

To Leon and Sylvia (my two biggest cheerleaders) for their constant love, support, and faith in me. Thank you for pushing me past my boundaries.

To the Kidlets (Jazmine, Erika, LJ, Arriana, and Nicholas), who made me believe that it was possible for me to be more.

To Beverly, for the editing, graphics suggestions, and never-ending pats on the back.

To Charles G, for beating every available (and unavailable) bush, and helping more than you realize.

To Reecie-Man, Shorty, and Wade F. – I wish you were here for me to share all of this with you.

To God, most of all, whose inspiration on the plane from Calgary made this whole project possible. I have truly experienced the fullness and glory of the truth that is, "What you focus on, expands." For that, and more, I am eternally grateful.

The book is also dedicated to you, the Reader, who will benefit from this resource if you choose to use and apply it. Know that there is always a solution available, even in the darkest times.

Table of Contents

Introduction

Congratulations! You have begun the process of taking control of your financial situation! You have taken an amazing step towards financial security – this workbook will assist you in taking further steps to discover the solution that is right for you while educating you about the process of foreclosure.

Financial difficulties are a common problem. People find themselves in situations that are beyond their control that affect their lives and financial stability. Divorce, bankruptcy, job loss, illness, and changing economic conditions are only a few examples of life altering situations that affect our finances.

If you are more than three payments behind in your mortgage payments, your lender or bank has probably already started foreclosure proceedings against you. When it comes to the subject of foreclosure, however, most homeowners are left in the dark. They have no idea where to turn for basic, credible, instructional information about the process and what to do in their situations. Internet searches for foreclosure information provide resources for investors to capitalize on the market. Foreclosure "help" resources are available, but hard to navigate through at the last minute. Conversely, property owners are bombarded with an increased amount of communication from "one-solution" sources – investors offer to buy their homes, lawyers offer bankruptcy services, mortgage brokers offer refinance options and sub prime lending.

Homeowners in distress have basic questions they want answered about the foreclosure process:

- What options do I have when facing foreclosure?
- What is a Redemption Period?
- How many days do I have to reinstate my loan?
- What is a Short Sale, and does it work in my favor?
- What is a Deed-in-Lieu of Foreclosure?
- Who do I turn to for help?

This Guide will empower you to take control of your rights and to identify the solution that meets your needs thereby giving you the means to save your property from foreclosure. That's right – YOU CAN TAKE CONTROL! This workbook is a means to assist you step by step, and will cover the following topics:

- The basics of the foreclosure process
- Explanation of common foreclosure terms
- Checklists and worksheets to assess your current situation
- The options you have when facing foreclosure
- Resources and contacts

Action needs to be taken immediately! If you are delinquent with your house payments, this Guide will provide you with the means of solving your problem now. Even if foreclosure action has been filed, you still have plenty of time. There are approved solutions that allow you rectify your situation, but you must act now. This Guide is easy to understand, and will provide you with the resources you need to save your home.

"People go from denial to despair without pausing on the intermediate step of actually doing something about the problem"

Former Vice President Al Gore, "An Inconvenient Truth"

WARNING! DO NOT SKIP AHEAD!

We realize that it's a large guide. However, the following sections are designed to take you through a specific and action-oriented process. Becoming impatient is detrimental to your circumstances!
Take the time to complete each section thoroughly!

The Basics of Foreclosure

In this section, you will learn about the foreclosure process, general terms, and common alternatives and pitfalls.

Preparation

In this section, you will review your personal financial situation, organize your paperwork, and begin asking yourself the tough questions. You will need to understand your personal situation PRIOR to contacting your lender (or any third party).

Contacting Your Lender

After you have organized your information and taken stock of your circumstances, you will then contact your lender to discuss what options they are prepared to offer. In this section, you will discuss forbearance agreements, payment options, law firm referrals, and deadline dates.

What Are Your Options?

Now that you have found out the hard numbers and dates from your lender, you can assess what options are available to you. In this section, you will review – in detail – the options that can be instituted immediately.

Choosing Options & Taking Action!

After completing all the worksheets and reviewing the choices you have available to you, it is time to make an informed decision and choose the options (yes, more than one!) that are best for your situation.

Section One:
The Basics of Foreclosure

Section One: The Basics of Foreclosure

Before beginning the process of understanding your personal financial situation, we will start to understand more about foreclosure. The following section explains the basic process of foreclosure, including types, timelines, consequences, and alternatives.

What is Foreclosure?

Foreclosure is the legal proceeding in which a bank or other secured creditor sells or repossesses a parcel of real property (immovable property) due to the owner's failure to comply with an agreement between the lender and borrower called a "mortgage" or "deed of trust".

Commonly, the violation of the mortgage is a default in payment of a promissory note, secured by a lien on the property. When the process is complete, it is typically said that "the lender has foreclosed its mortgage or lien."

Why Lenders Foreclose

Lenders will begin foreclosure proceedings for the following reasons:

- No payment/excessive late payments
- Transfer of title without notification or permission
- Threat to Junior Mortgagee if First mortgage is delinquent

It is important to understand that banks and mortgage companies DO NOT want your house. They want the payments that have been agreed upon – they do not want to take a property into their inventory. This is why they will make all attempts to work out a solution to your current payment difficulties before beginning foreclosure procedures.

Types of Foreclosure

Each state in the U.S. handles its real estate foreclosures differently, and it is important to understand those differences and know your specific state's procedures. The terms used and timeframes vary greatly from state to state, but the following information provides a general overview of the different processes and considerations. To find out general information about your particular state, see the **Procedures by State** section at the back of the workbook.

Judicial Foreclosures   vs.   Non-Judicial Foreclosures

Judicial foreclosures are processed through the courts, beginning with the lender filing a complaint and recording a notice of Lis Pendens. The complaint will state what the debt is, and why the default should allow the lender to foreclose and take the property given as security. The homeowner will be served notice of the complaint, either by mailing, direct service, or publication of the notice, and will have the opportunity to be heard before the court. If the court finds the debt valid, and in default, it will issue a judgment for the total amount owed, including the costs of the foreclosure process.

After the judgment has been entered, a writ will be issued by the court authorizing a sheriff's sale. The sheriff's sale is an auction, open to anyone, and is held in a public place, which can range from in front of the courthouse steps, to in front of the property being auctioned. Sheriff's sales will require either cash to be paid at the time of sale, or a substantial deposit, with the balance paid from later that same day up to 30 days after the sale. At the end of the auction, the highest bidder will be the owner of the property, subject to the court's confirmation of the sale. After the court has confirmed the sale, a sheriff's deed will be prepared and delivered to the highest bidder. When that deed is recorded, the highest bidder is the owner of the property.

Non-judicial foreclosures are processed without court intervention, with the requirements for the foreclosure established by state statutes. Non-Judicial foreclosures are possible due to a "Power of Sale" clause in the mortgage or deed of trust.

When a loan default occurs, the homeowner will be mailed a default letter, and in many states, a Notice of Default will be recorded at approximately the same time. If the homeowner does not cure the default, a Notice of Sale will be mailed to the homeowner, posted in public places, recorded at the county recorder's office, and published in area legal publications. After the legally required time period has expired, a public auction will be held, with the highest bidder becoming the owner of the property, subject to their receipt and recordation of the deed. Auctions of non-judicial foreclosures will generally require cash, or cash equivalent either at the sale, or very shortly thereafter.

It is important to note that each non-judicial foreclosure state has different procedures. Some do not require a Notice of Default, but start with a Notice of Sale. Others require only the publication of the Notice of Sale to announce the sale, with no direct owner notification required. See your state's website for further procedural information.

Foreclosure Process

The foreclosure process is actually a two-part action: Pre-foreclosure and Formal Foreclosure.

Pre-Foreclosure:
1. The homeowner misses a few payments.
2. The lender sends the homeowner late notices. If they fail to receive a response or bring the payments current, the lender attempts contact (by phone or mail) to rectify the situation.
3. If payments are not made, the loan is transferred to the Loss Mitigation department, and a payment arrangement is proposed.
4. If the payment arrangements are not accepted and/or adhered to, the lender invokes the acceleration clause and demands payment in full.

Formal Foreclosure:
1. The lender transfers the collection to a law firm, and begins formal foreclosure proceedings.
2. Legal notices regarding the attempt to collect a debt are published in local publications.
3. The allotted timeframe elapses without an agreement on a satisfactory financial solution, and the date for the auction is set.
4. Legal notice and advertisements of the actual foreclosure sale are posted in local publications.
5. On the date of auction, the house is sold to the highest bidder. If the house is not sold, the lender takes possession of the property.
6. If the homeowner is still living in the property, the lender or new owner can begin eviction proceedings.
7. If the house is sold for less than is owed, the homeowner is notified of the outstanding debt (a deficiency judgment).

After a Foreclosure Sale

Money Distribution
When a house is sold at auction or at a Sheriff's Sale, there is an order in which debts and liens are paid.

1. Real Estate Taxes and IRS Liens
2. First Mortgage
3. Second/Third Mortgage
4. Lien Holders or Attached Creditors
5. The Homeowner (if there is a surplus amount)

Redemption Periods

After a foreclosure has taken place, some states have a redemption period – a period of time established by state law during which a property owner has the right to redeem his or her property from a forced, public foreclosure sale. See the **Procedures by State** section at the back of the workbook to determine if your state has a redemption period for foreclosed properties.

Consequences of Foreclosure

Foreclosure is extremely damaging to your credit rating and financial future. Some of the consequences are:

- **Loss of property** – you WILL lose your property if the foreclosure process goes through the complete cycle. The property will be sold at auction or repossessed by the bank.

- **Loss of equity** – you WILL lose the equity you have built up in your home. Equity is the property's current value minus the sum of all liens against it. If you bought your home for $150,000, and the current value is $200,000, the equity (cash) value is $50,000. That cash will be gone if your house is lost to foreclosure.

- **Damaged credit rating** – a foreclosure is worse on your credit rating than a Bankruptcy; it says to a credit lender that you made no attempt to fix your situation! You will need to be prepared to pay cash or high interest rates for anything that requires credit – an immediate apartment, a future house, car, even a cell phone.

- **Possible loss of employment** – if you have a job that requires a security clearance or a responsible financial background, a foreclosure is detrimental to your employment.

- **Possible deficiency judgment** – if the house is sold at auction for less than is owed, you are then responsible for the monetary difference. So, even though the house is no longer in your possession, the lender can still come after you by filing a deficiency judgment for the amount that was not collected.

What You Should Know About Foreclosure

Financial difficulties are a common problem. People find themselves in situations that are beyond their control that affect their lives and financial stability. The following are only a few examples of life altering situations that affect our finances:

- Death of Borrower
- Unemployment
- Increased Expenses
- Salary Reduction
- Incarceration
- Failure of Business
- Balloon Payment
- Decreased Earnings (self-employed)

- Underinsured
- Natural Disaster
- Disability or Health-Related Expenses
- Loss of Overtime or Second Job
- Poor Financial Management Skills
- Involuntary Relocation
- Bankruptcy
- Creative Mortgages (cases of "Too Much House")

Facing foreclosure can be a stressful, emotional process. Even if the signs of financial trouble are clearly approaching, many homeowners find it easier to avoid the situation rather than deal with the whole truth. This is a common mistake, and one that can be detrimental to your situation. When faced with the possibility of losing their home, many homeowners may feel...

- Stressed
- Vulnerable
- Uneducated about the foreclosure process
- Unsure about the condition of their home

- Overwhelmed
- Inundated
- Uninformed about the reality of real estate transactions
- Embarrassed about their current financial situation

Under these circumstances, a homeowner may exhibit some of the following behaviors:

- They may not want to open their mail or answer the telephone.
- They may seek assistance from anyone offering a solution, even if the solution may not be right for their individual circumstance.
- They may be unwilling to listen to any advice because of their emotional attachment to the home.
- They may be waiting on someone else to provide a solution without being willing to initiate any action themselves.
- They may not be willing to discuss the situation with others who are affected by the foreclosure, such as a spouse or co-borrower.
- They may be embarrassed about the situation and resentful of involvement by third-parties.
- They may proceed through life in complete denial until the last possible moment.

Although this behavior is understood, it is not healthy or proactive. By purchasing this workbook, you have made a step in the right direction. No matter how overwhelmed you may feel, the information provided on this workbook will assist you in taking control of your financial future. You MUST take action before it is too late.

After completing the worksheets, you will be in a position to accurately assess your situation and options. We will guide you through the process of organizing your paperwork, understanding your current financial outlook, communicating with your lenders, and choosing the options that are best for your individual situation.

Alternatives to Foreclosure

(Provided by the Department of Housing and Urban Development)

First and foremost, DO NOT IGNORE THE LETTERS FROM YOUR LENDER. Communication is key – if you are having problems making your payments, call or write to your lender's Loss Mitigation Department without delay. Explain your situation. The information in this workbook will prepare you to provide them with financial information, such as your monthly income and expenses. Without this information, they may not be able to help.

Secondly, stay in your home. You may not qualify for assistance if you abandon your property.

Every lender's policy is to evaluate individual circumstances as soon as possible. Individual cases are reviewed based on the following conditions:

- Reason for default
- Borrower's attitude towards the debt
- Whether the delinquency is temporary or permanent

When working with your lender to find a financial solution, you may be considered for the following seven options (**these alternatives are reviewed in further detail in Section Four**):

1. Temporary Indulgence. This is a grace period, usually 30 to 60 days, which may be granted to bring the mortgage current. If you request a Temporary Indulgence, you will need to demonstrate evidence that warrants the grace period. An indulgence is considered to be appropriate in the following situations:

- A contract for sale has been ratified and a closing date can be verified.
- An insurance settlement
- Pending receipt of approved funding (refinance)

2. Military Indulgence. A civilian borrower who later enters the military is entitled to Military Indulgence granted under the terms of the Soldiers' and Sailors' Civil Relief Act. There are two components of this provision:

- **Interest Rate Reduction:** FNMA (Fannie Mae) policy requires a reduction in the interest rate from the time the borrower begins active duty to the date of release at the current rate of 6% (rate may be subject to change). This benefit is retroactive should the borrower notify the lender sometime after beginning active duty.

- **Additional Forbearance:** In certain cases related to the financial hardship usually associated with the loss of greater civilian pay, the veteran may request special consideration in the form of a reduction in the monthly mortgage. The difference between the original monthly mortgage amount and the reduced payment is referred to as "arrearage". Upon release from active duty, the borrower would be responsible for bringing the arrearage current.

3. Special Forbearance. Your lender may be able to arrange a repayment plan based on your financial situation and may even provide for a temporary reduction or suspension of your payments. You may qualify for this if you have recently experienced a reduction in income or an increase in living expenses. You must furnish information to your lender to show that you would be able to meet the requirements of the new payment plan.

4. Mortgage Modification. If your income has been unexpectedly reduced and you cannot pay the current mortgage amount, but you could pay a smaller amount, you may qualify for a mortgage modification. You may be able to refinance the debt and/or extend the term of your mortgage loan. This may help you catch up by reducing the monthly payments to a more affordable level. You will need to qualify by submitting proof of your reduced income and ability to pay a lesser loan payment.

5. Partial Claim. This applies to FHA mortgages only - your lender may be able to work with you to obtain a one-time payment from the FHA-Insurance fund to bring your mortgage current. You may qualify for a Partial Claim if:

- Your loan is at least 4 months delinquent but no more than 12 months delinquent;
- You are able to begin making full mortgage payments.

When your lender files a Partial Claim, the U.S. Department of Housing and Urban Development will pay your lender the amount necessary to bring your mortgage current. You must execute a Promissory Note, and a Lien will be placed on your property until the Promissory Note is paid in full.

The Promissory Note is interest-free and is due when you pay off the first mortgage or when you sell the property.

6. Short Sale. If your house is not worth more than what you currently owe, the lender may allow a short sale. This will allow you to avoid foreclosure by selling your property on the market for an amount less than the amount necessary to pay off your mortgage loan. You may qualify for a property short sale if:

- The loan is at least 2 months delinquent;
- You are able to sell your house within 3 to 5 months; and
- A new appraisal (that your lender will obtain) shows that the value of your home is less than the mortgage amount.

There is a specific process that must be followed <u>to the letter</u> if you are going to submit a short sale package to your lender for acceptance. Again, a short sale MUST be approved by the lender prior to selling your home. You will need to work with your lender's Loss Mitigation department to obtain the criteria for approval.

7. Deed-in-Lieu of Foreclosure. As a last resort, you may be able to voluntarily "give back" your property to the lender. This won't save your house, but it is not as damaging to your credit rating as a foreclosure. You can qualify for a deed-in-lieu of foreclosure if:

- You are in default and don't qualify for any of the other options;
- Your attempts at selling the house before foreclosure were unsuccessful; and
- You don't have another mortgage in default.

<u>Some of these options are only available to you if you are still living in the home</u>. Your lender or a qualified housing counselor (see Resources and Contacts) will determine if you qualify for any of the alternatives. Most lenders will not object to any reasonable plan, provided it does not compromise the lien position or come into conflict with any other policy or commitment.

Important Points!

It is very important that you open communication with your lenders at the first sign of financial difficulty in order to take advantages of the assistance they will offer you. Be completely honest and forthcoming about your situation. If you agree to a delinquency cure, be sure you can comply and be faithful to your commitment. If there is a change in your circumstances, and you cannot honor your agreement, contact your lender immediately.

If your situation is expected to be long term, it would be useless and in bad faith to negotiate a delinquency cure. If you cannot afford your house, DO NOT KEEP IT. The stress of attempting to keep up with payments is truly detrimental to your personal life.

Seller Beware!

Foreclosure is a matter of public record. When a foreclosure is announced, a homeowner will receive countless letters containing offers from investors, mortgage brokers, bankruptcy attorneys, and additional service agents. <u>Carefully investigate all offers presented to you</u>. Solutions that sound too simple or too good to be true usually are.

If you're selling your home without professional guidance, beware of buyers who try to rush you through the process. Unfortunately, there are people who may try to take advantage of your financial situation. Financially or emotionally distressed homeowners often become the unwitting victims of unethical practitioners who seek to exploit the misfortune of others.

There are several precautions you can take to avoid being taken advantage of:

- Don't sign any papers you don't fully understand.
- Make sure you get all "promises" in writing.
- Beware of any loan assumption where you are not formally released from liability for your mortgage debt.
- Check with a lawyer or your mortgage company before entering into any deal involving your home.
- If you are selling the house yourself to avoid foreclosure, check to see if there are any complaints against the prospective buyer. You can contact your state's Attorney General, the State Real Estate Commission, or the local District Attorney's Consumer Fraud Unit for this type of information.

Here are the states (as of the date of publication) that have been enacted to protect homeowners from foreclosure scams:

Michigan	Minnesota	Maryland
Illinois	Colorado	California
Georgia	Missouri	New York
Rhode Island	Washington	Florida

Other states (such as the District of Columbia) have introduced bills similar to the ones above. If your state has not yet considered a bill such as these, call your legislator. This is a VERY public issue... they will listen!

Common Foreclosure Scams

FACT: Foreclosure is a matter of public record, and CANDY to investors, attorneys, mortgage brokers, and foreclosure consultants. The homeowner often thinks, "Can't we keep this private? I don't want my neighbors/family/coworkers/church members/babysitter/significant other/dog walker's sister's cousin to know about my financial situation"!

Once your bank goes public with your foreclosure situation, however, it is no longer a private matter. You will be inundated with phone calls, letters, and various forms of solicitation offering to save your home. Some are legitimate offers – some are strictly misinformation from individuals whose goal is to take your equity and get your home. **THESE ARE THE VULTURES**. You've probably already been approached by a few of them, telling you that your only chance to stop foreclosure is to sell the house (usually to them, quick-fast-and-in-a-hurry, and for a lot less than it's worth – right?). Or worse: while pretending to help you they try to con you into a far worse scam.

(Just a note, here... NOT ALL BANKERS, INVESTORS, CONSULTANTS, OR LENDERS ARE VULTURES! However, there is a bad element in the real estate business that is out to take advantage of you and profit from your current situation.)

This is usually how it starts:

As soon as news of your foreclosure is made public, the flood of letters and phone calls begin, and the vultures are on the hunt. Some of them are less polished with their approach: you may receive a sloppy letter offering to help out by buying your home. Others may call you on the phone (ignoring the "Do Not Call List" rules and regulations) or even knock on the door and offer their services. These are the amateurs – probably fresh out of a beginning real estate investor class. They can be safely disregarded.

The dangerous ones are the **Vultures in Sheep's Clothing**.

A Vulture in Sheep's Clothing...

These are the slick, polished "professionals" who offer to assist you. They will hand you a savvy business card, listen intently and console you over a cup of coffee or glass of water at your kitchen table, all the while assuring you that they'll stop your foreclosure regardless of your situation. Heck, they'll even promise to let you stay in your home! All you have to do is sign on the dotted line...

Does that sound familiar? Unfortunately, this promise, in some instances, is too good to be true. **Don't ignore your inner sense of protection** – if it sounds too good to be true, it could be a scam designed to steal your equity.

While some of the solutions presented are valid options in certain instances, some investors have <u>no intention</u> of letting you stay in the property – at least, not for very long. Read the contracts they present – they are heavily weighed in their favor, and the slightest infraction on your part will let them evict you and walk away with your property and your equity (especially in landlord-friendly states!).

Again, read any contracts presented to you. An upstanding investor should not have a problem allowing you take a day or two to review the documentation with a professional. If they are pushing you to sign right now, it could be a scam.

Let's review the most common scams that vultures will use to steal your home:

The Leaseback
Unfortunately, the Leaseback is one of the most popular of the foreclosure scams, because it fills the most common need of the homeowner in distress – the desire to stay in the home they have built.

The Leaseback is also referred to as "selling your home and renting it back" or just "a rent-back option". The scam works like this:

- You deed your home to an investor.
- You sign a rental agreement.
- The investor may offer you an option of buying the house back in the future (for a higher price than you sold it to them).
- The investor takes over the payments – they may even bring your loan current.
- The investor pockets the rent you pay.
- The investor waits for you to make a mistake.

The slightest mistake, and you are evicted IMMEDIATELY. If you fail to pay your rent on time, or are one penny off the agreed-upon payment amount, you are evicted. If the lease says you cannot hang pictures on the wall, and you hang a photo of your beloved pet, Skippy, you are evicted. If the rental agreement says you need to hand-deliver the rental payment, but you decide to mail it, you are evicted. Any diversion from the lease, you are out on the street. You are legally obligated to leave.

A leaseback, while not always advantageous to the homeowner, is not illegal. There are some states (Maryland, Colorado, Illinois, and Minnesota), however, who have strict regulations to how a leaseback must be structured and documented. Any violation of those regulations, and the vulture is caught!

The Escrow Loan

When you think of "escrow", you think "safety" and "security", correct?

Wikipedia.com defines escrow as a legal arrangement in which an asset (often money, but sometimes other property such as a deed of title) is delivered to a third party (called an escrow agent) to be held in trust pending a contingency or the fulfillment of a condition or conditions in a contract, such as payment of a purchase price. Upon that event occurring, the escrow agent will deliver the asset to the proper recipient, otherwise the escrow agent is bound by his or her fiduciary duty to maintain the escrow account.

In a foreclosure scam, however, a "deed in escrow loan" provides the exact opposite of safety and security.

Here's how the scam works:

- An investor offers to provide you with a loan to bring your loan current.
- You sign over the deed to your home.
- The deed is held in escrow (the investor will explain that this protects his investment and keeps their costs low).
- You begin to make payments on the loan.

If you're a day late with the payment, the investor will record the deed and evict you. You may not have documentation to prove that you were lent any money, but the investor CERTAINLY has a deed – signed by you – that proves you sold them your home.

If someone wants to lend you money to bring your loan current, sign a promissory note and give them weekly or monthly payments that you can afford. Any other lending scenario is probably presented by someone who does not have a license to lend money and is trying to get around state and/or federal lending practices. Are you willing to trust your most valuable asset – your home – to someone like this? Think about that.

Trust Agreements

The Trust Agreement scam is similar in nature to the Escrow scenario.

What is a Trust? Wikipedia.com defines a trust as an arrangement whereby money or property is owned and managed by one person (or persons, or organizations) for the benefit of another. A trust is created by a Settlor, who entrusts some or all of his property to people of his choice (the Trustees). The trustees are the legal owners of the trust property, but they are obliged to hold the property for the benefit of one or more individuals or organizations (the Beneficiary), usually specified by the settlor.

Here's how the scam plays out:

- Investor offers to bring your loan current.
- Investor charges $1000 (or a similar amount) to pay all legal fees for setting up a trust.
- The trust is set up as "66 Lincoln Street Jones Family Trust" (assuming your name is "Jones", and you live at 66 Lincoln Street).
- The deed names the investor's company (ABC Investments, Inc.) as the Trustee.
- The deal is structured so that once the loan is repaid (plus a management fee), the trust will then deed the house back to you.

Can you see the scam working? In this scenario, it is very easy for an investor to put you at ease and use "trust" to con you out of your home. You assume that because the trust is named for your home and family, you have a controlling interest. In truth, ABC Investments, Inc, controls the trust, and THE TRUST NOW OWNS THE HOME. You have just given your property away, but you are still obligated to pay for it. Miss a loan payment? You are evicted, and you have no legal ramification, because you no longer own the home.

Equity Stripping

Have you ever heard of Equity Stripping? It can be done in two ways – both very scary, both leaving you, the homeowner, with little to none of the equity you've worked so hard to build.

The first technique involves an investor and an unlawful appraiser:
- Unscrupulous appraiser creates a report stating that you house is worth more than its current value.
- Investor gets you to refinance.
- Cash is paid to the investor at closing.
- The process is repeated.

Initially, your payments may drop, but your loan balance increases due to high fees and repeated refinancing. The equity you had built up is being paid out in cash during each closing. This scam is primarily for homeowners who have a large amount of equity in their homes.

The second technique works similar to a Leaseback:
- You deed your home to an investor.
- You sign a rental agreement.
- The investor may offer you an option of buying the house back in the future (for a higher price than you sold it to them).
- The investor pockets the rent you pay.
- THE INVESTOR NEVER MAKES A PAYMENT...

... and you have no idea until you receive another threatening letter from the mortgage company asking for their money. The investor has been cashing your rent checks, and has not made a payment on your mortgage loan.

At this point, I want to mention again that, even though we use the term "vultures" and are painting some very scary scenarios, not all investors, mortgage brokers, realtors, or foreclosure consultants are deceitful. Not everyone who comes to you offering assistance is unscrupulous. It IS important, however, to be informed of the scams that are out there so you can protect your home. Forewarned is forearmed!

Foreclosure Mediators
Because DFCS, Inc. is a Foreclosure Consulting service, this particular scam grates on our nerves more than most. This group of vultures gives the business a bad name, and the way they take advantage of the homeowner in distress is truly inexcusable.

Foreclosure Mediators make promises of negotiation and home salvage, but are really in it for the money you pay up front. The scam follows this trail:

- You contact a Foreclosure Mediation service and submit an application.
- They "review your file" (usually within 24-48 hours).
- They inform you that, for an upfront fee, they can assist you by structuring a forbearance agreement with your lender or negotiating a smaller payment, no matter what your foreclosure situation is.
- You submit paperwork and your NON-REFUNDABLE fee... and wait.

In this case, they have what they want from you – the upfront payment. If you attempt to follow up with them and actually get someone on the phone, they will tell you that the fee you paid was enough to get the ball rolling, but it's a hard process filled with lots of red tape. They may say that your bank refused their workout proposal, and that's the end of it. They MAY say that the process will take longer than expected, and more money is needed to finish the negotiations. Whether you pay more money or give up at this point, the money that you have paid to the company is gone.

Predatory Loans

Predatory lenders promise loans that are "too good to be true" and pressure borrowers to take them on the spot. However, did you know that it is illegal to loan money to someone that you suspect cannot afford to repay the funds? Illegal or not, the goal for predatory lenders is not to receive the excessive payments you make – it's the hope that you DON'T make the payment so they can take your home.

Here's a few things you should know about spotting and avoid predatory loans. The Center for Responsible Lending in Durham, North Carolina, has outlined the seven signs of predatory lending:

- **Excessive Fees:** Points and fees are costs not directly reflected in interest rates. Because these costs can be financed, they are easy to disguise or downplay. On competitive loans, fees below 1% of the loan amount are typical. On predatory loans, fees totaling more than 5% of the loan amount are common.

- **Abusive Prepayment Penalties:** Borrowers with higher-interest sub-prime loans have a strong incentive to refinance as soon as their credit improves. However, up to 80% of all sub-prime mortgages carry a prepayment penalty – a fee for paying off a loan early. An abusive prepayment penalty typically is effective more than three years and/or costs more than six months' interest. In the prime market, only about 2% of home loans carry prepayment penalties of any length.

- **Kickbacks to Brokers (yield spread premiums):** When brokers deliver a loan with an inflated interest rate (i.e., higher than the rate acceptable to the lender), the lender often pays a "yield spread premium" – a kickback for making the loan more costly to the borrower.

- **Loan Flipping:** A lender "flips" a borrower by refinancing a loan to generate fee income without providing any net tangible benefit to the borrower. Flipping can quickly drain borrower equity and increase monthly payments – sometimes on homes that had previously been owned free of debt.

- **Unnecessary Products:** Sometimes borrowers may pay more than necessary because lenders sell and finance unnecessary insurance or other products along with the loan.

- **Mandatory Arbitration:** Some loan contracts require "mandatory arbitration," meaning that the borrowers are not allowed to seek legal remedies in a court if they find that their home is threatened by loans with illegal or abusive terms. Mandatory arbitration makes it much less likely that borrowers will receive fair and appropriate remedies in cases of wrongdoing.

- **Steering & Targeting:** Predatory lenders may steer borrowers into sub-prime mortgages, even when the borrowers could qualify for a mainstream loan. Vulnerable borrowers may be subjected to aggressive sales tactics and sometimes outright fraud. Fannie Mae has estimated that up to half of borrowers with sub-prime mortgages could have qualified for loans with better terms.

How can you protect yourself from predatory lending?

- Always shop around.
- Ask questions.
- If you don't understand the loan terms, talk to someone you trust to look at the documents for you.
- Don't trust ads promising "No Credit? No Problem!"
- Ignore high-pressure sales tactics.
- Don't take the first loan you are offered.
- Remember that a low monthly payment isn't always a 'deal.' Look at the TOTAL cost of the loan.
- Be wary of promises to refinance the loan to a better rate in the future.
- Never sign a blank document or anything the lender promised to fill in later.

Final Thoughts

We have discussed a variety of diabolical schemes. At this point, I have just two more words for you – **DON'T PANIC!**

Most vultures prey on your confusion, miseducation, and high stress level. They are waiting to take advantage of your lack of time, money, patience, and knowledge of the system – at your greatest point of confusion, they will present an offer that looks great on the surface, but had a hidden agenda underneath.

Thankfully, there's plenty of good news to consider.

First, to be fair to the GOOD apples in the bunch, not all Investors, Mortgage Bankers, Foreclosure Consultants, or Realtors are vultures. Secondly, not all scenarios offered to you are illegal or immoral. For example:

- An investor CAN rent your house back to you – ensure the terms are beneficial and you fully understand the lease violations.
- A company CAN provide you with a sub-prime loan to refinance your home - not all sub-prime loans are predatory. Ensure that you are not pressured into a loan you cannot afford.
- A company CAN lend you money to bring your loan current – ensure that you are not signing a document you do not understand and receive legal counsel if you are unsure of the agreement.
- A third party CAN take over the payments for your house – ensure the penalties for a missed payment do not solely fall upon your shoulders.

There are many viable solutions that will be offered to you. As long as you review all the documentation and the benefit to you COMPLETELY and THOROUGHLY, vultures do not stand a chance with you and your property.

Next Steps

Now that you have read about the foreclosure process, it is time for the do-it-yourself portion of the workbook. The worksheets and information will lead you to making the right decision for your individual circumstance.

The following sections will take you through a specific and action-oriented process:

Preparation

In this section, you will review your personal financial situation, organize your paperwork, and begin asking yourself the tough questions. You will need to understand your personal situation PRIOR to contacting your lender (or any third party).

Contacting Your Lender

After you have organized your information and taken stock of your circumstances, you will then contact your lender to discuss what options they are prepared to offer. In this section, you will discuss forbearance agreements, payment options, law firm referrals, and deadline dates.

What Are Your Options?

Now that you have found out the hard numbers and dates from your lender, you can assess what options are available to you. In this section, you will review – in detail – the eight options that can be instituted immediately.

Choosing Options & Taking Action!

After completing all the worksheets and reviewing the choices you have available to you, it is time to make an informed decision and choose the options (yes, more than one!) that are best for your situation.

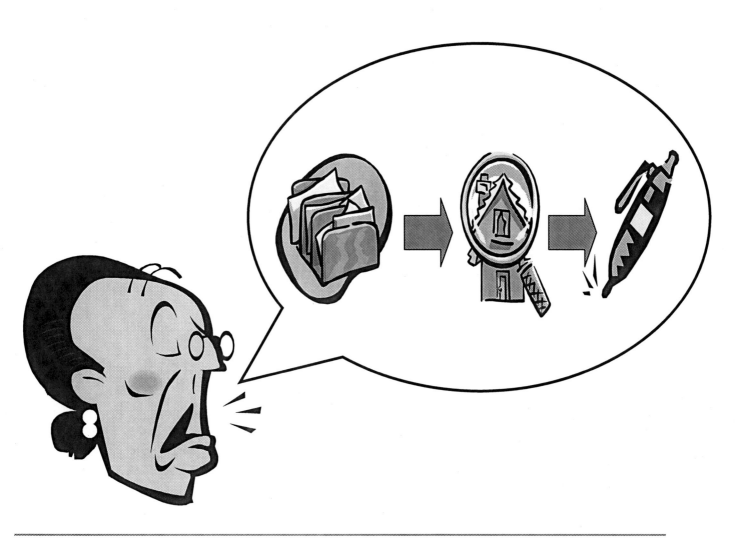

Section Two:
Preparation

Section Two: Preparation

In this section, you will prepare for your communication with your lender by gathering and reviewing all personal financial information, correspondence, and relevant notes.

You MUST be very thorough during this process – be prepared to look through tons of information to extract the most recent data you will need for the following worksheets. DO NOT SKIP A STEP.

First and foremost, gather together all of your mail and open every letter. You will need all communication from your lender and/or representative law firm.

Gather ALL of the following information (check all that apply) and separate into the following piles or folders:

☐ Pile 1: <u>Most Recent</u> Communication from Mortgage Companies, Banks, Law Firms, IRS, etc.

☐ Pile 2: Lender Information – 1st Mortgage

☐ Pile 3: Lender Information – 2nd Mortgage

☐ Pile 4: Law Firm Information

☐ Pile 5: IRS Notices

☐ Pile 6: Employment W2's or 1099's

☐ Pile 7: Checking/Savings Account Statements (last three months)

☐ Pile 8: Tax Returns (last two years)

☐ Pile 9: Disability/Government Assistance Letters

☐ Pile 10: Utility Bills

☐ Pile 11: Homeowner/Condo Association Bills

☐ Pile 12: Create separate piles for Investor, Attorney (Bankruptcy), Refinance and Realtor postcards and letters. <u>You will need these</u>!

Assess Your Current Situation

In order to create a clear and accurate plan of action, first and foremost, you must determine your current circumstances and understand your complete financial picture. This enables you to accurately assess the options available to you.

This information is for your eyes only, so be as accurate and truthful as possible.

Loan Type   ☐ FHA ☐ VA ☐ Bank

Credit   ☐ Excellent   For your most recent credit information, contact the three main credit bureaus (Equifax, Experian, and TransUnion) for a copy of your credit report. Most times, you will be able to obtain the information for free. Contact information is in the Resources section of the workbook.

                       ☐ Good

                       ☐ Fair

                       ☐ Poor

                       FICO Score: _____

Monthly Income   ☐ Full Time Income $ _____

                       ☐ Part Time Income $ _____

                       ☐ Unemployment Income $ _____

                       ☐ Child Support $ _____

                       ☐ Alimony $ _____

                       ☐ Disability $ _____

                       ☐ Other $ _____

Current Situation (continued)

Monthly Expenses

☐ Other Mortgages/Liens $ _____

☐ Auto Loan(s) $ _____

☐ Auto Insurance $ _____

☐ Auto Expenses $ _____

☐ Credit Cards/Loans $ _____

☐ Health/Medical $ _____

☐ Child Support/Alimony $ _____

☐ Utilities/Phone $ _____

☐ Food/Spending Money $ _____

☐ Other $ _____

Assets

☐ Home Value $ _____

☐ Other Real Estate $ _____

☐ Checking Account(s) $ _____

☐ Savings Account(s) $ _____

☐ Car(s) $ _____

☐ IRA/Keogh Account(s) $ _____

☐ 401k/ESPO Account(s) $ _____

☐ Stocks/Bonds/CDs $ _____

☐ Other $ _____

Current Situation (continued)

Additional Questions

Is there a Co-Borrower listed on the property? □ Yes □ No

Name:

_____

_____

_____

Do you currently occupy the property? □ Yes □ No

If No, is the property a rental? □ Yes □ No

Rental Income:

$ _____

Is the property currently listed for sale? □ Yes □ No

Agent Name:

_____

Agent Phone:

_____

Have you contacted a credit counseling agency for assistance? □ Yes □ No

Counselor Firm:

_____

Counselor Name/Phone:

_____

Do you pay real estate taxes? □ Yes □ No

Are the taxes current? □ Yes □ No

Amount Owed:

$ _____

Are there any additional liens on the property? □ Yes □ No

Total Amount Owed:

$ _____

Current Situation (continued)

Have you formally filed for
Bankruptcy?

☐ Yes ☐ No

Type:

☐ Chapter 7

☐ Chapter 13

Filing Date:

_____

Attorney Name:

_____

Attorney Phone:

_____

**Do not proceed until the previous
worksheet is completed.**

Financial Information Sheet

Property Information	
Bedrooms/Bathrooms	
Levels	
Basement	
Square Footage/Style	
Year Built	
What is the condition of your home?	Scale from 1 (Poor) – 10 (Excellent) : ____
Financial Information	
If Selling, Desired Sale Amount	
"Least Acceptable" Sale Amount	
Total Debt	
Cash Needed	
Mortgage Holder – 1st	Company:
Monthly Payment:	Account No:
HOA Fee:	Contact Name:
Interest Rate:	Address:
Months Past Due:	Phone:
Mortgage Holder – 2nd	Company:
Monthly Payment:	Account No:
Interest Rate:	Contact Name:
Months Past Due:	Address:
	Phone:
Comparable Home Values *	$
Appraised Value	$
Area Rental Rates	$

* Comparable Values for real estate must be for houses of the same type/size/features (same amount of bedrooms, square footage, immediate neighborhood, etc.)

Home Information Sheet

Basic Home Information	
Condition of the House	Scale from 1 (Poor) – 10 (Excellent) : ____
Condition of Grounds	Scale from 1 (Poor) – 10 (Excellent) : ____
What is the condition of the neighboring properties?	Scale from 1 (Poor) – 10 (Excellent) : ____
Is the home habitable?	☐ Yes ☐ No
Does the foundation need repair?	☐ Yes ☐ No
Does the roof need to be replaced?	☐ Yes ☐ No
Exterior type?	
Exterior Repairs?	
Type of parking/size & condition of parking spaces	
# of Windows	
Total # of rooms	
Do the rooms need repainting?	☐ Yes ☐ No
# of rooms that need carpet	
# of rooms that need vinyl	
Do hardwood floors need refinishing?	☐ Yes ☐ No
Do bathrooms need cleaning, upgrade, or total remodel?	
Is there a basement? Is it finished?	
Is basement dry?	☐ Yes ☐ No

Basic Home Information	
What type of heat does the home have?	☐ Gas ☐ Oil ☐ Electric ☐ Radiator ☐ Forced Hot Air ☐ Baseboard ☐ Gravity
Condition of system?	Scale from 1 (Poor) – 10 (Excellent) : ____
Central air conditioning?	☐ Yes ☐ No
Circuit breaker or fuses?	
Condition of plumbing	Scale from 1 (Poor) – 10 (Excellent) : ____
Condition of water heater	Scale from 1 (Poor) – 10 (Excellent) : ____
What usable/updated appliances are included?	☐ Refrigerator ☐ Dishwasher ☐ Stove ☐ Oven ☐ Washer ☐ Dryer ☐ Microwave

Do not proceed until the previous worksheets are completed.

Explain Why You Are Currently Facing Foreclosure

Write a statement about why you are currently facing foreclosure. Your mortgage company and other companies will ask you for this information, so this sheet will help you begin to gather your thoughts and craft a clear explanation of your circumstances.

Do not be afraid to get personal, but please be truthful and as thorough as possible.

_____

_____

_____

_____

_____

_____

_____

_____

_____

_____

_____

_____

_____

_____

_____

_____

_____

_____

_____

_____

Immediate Issues and Life Goals

If foreclosed upon, where will you move?

_____

_____

_____

_____

_____

_____

_____

_____

_____

If foreclosed upon, how will you repair your credit?

_____

_____

_____

_____

_____

_____

_____

_____

_____

What other issues, challenges, or concerns are you currently dealing with?

_____

_____

_____

_____

_____

_____

_____

_____

_____

_____

What are your future life goals?

_____

_____

_____

_____

_____

_____

_____

_____

_____

_____

Recognizing that a Foreclosure is extremely damaging to your credit, how will it affect your immediate plans or future goals?

_____

_____

_____

_____

_____

_____

_____

_____

_____

_____

How will avoiding a Foreclosure affect your immediate plans or future goals?

_____

_____

_____

_____

_____

_____

_____

_____

_____

_____

_____

Ways to Make Extra Money...

Have you looked at ways to make extra money to tide you over or create an extra monthly income? Consider some of the following options for brining in extra cash to your household, and then take some time to write down some thoughts and ideas of your own.

Suggestions	Your Ideas
• Sell items on eBay or other Internet auction sites	
• Pawn items	
• Garage or yard sale	
• Take items to the flea market or consignment shop	
• Rent a room (or rooms) in your home	
• Rent out your entire home	
• Start an internet business	
• Start a network marketing business	
• Join an affiliate program and sell items	
• Take out a loan on your IRA	
• Take out a loan on your 401(K)	
• Take out a loan on your car title (only if automobile is paid off)	
• Create a physical side business (day care, cleaning services, etc.)	
• Obtain a second job (part time or full time)	

Section Checklist

Do not proceed until the following worksheets are completed:

- ☐ Assess Your Current Situation
- ☐ Financial Info Sheet
- ☐ Property Info Sheet
- ☐ Explanation of Why You Are Currently Facing Foreclosure
- ☐ Immediate Plans and Life Goals
- ☐ Ways to Make Extra Money...

Review: **OPEN ALL MAIL** and gather ALL of the following information (check all that apply) and separate into the following piles or folders:

- ☐ Most Recent Communication from Mortgage Companies, Banks, Law Firms, IRS, etc.
- ☐ Create separate piles for Investor, Attorney (Bankruptcy), Refinance and Realtor postcards and letters.
- ☐ Lender Information – 1st Mortgage
- ☐ Lender Information – 2nd Mortgage
- ☐ Law Firm Information
- ☐ IRS Notices
- ☐ Employment W2's or 1099's
- ☐ Checking/Savings Account Statements (last three months)
- ☐ Tax Returns (last two years)
- ☐ Disability/Government Assistance Letters
- ☐ Utility Bills
- ☐ Homeowner/Condo Association Bills
- ☐ Reinstatement Amount * $ _____
- ☐ Payoff Amount * $ _____

* Reinstatement Amount: The amount required to bring your loan current.
* Payoff Amount: the amount required to pay off the mortgage in full.

You will need to ask for BOTH amounts in your discussions with law firms and mortgage companies.

Do not proceed until the previous worksheets are completed.

Section Three:
Contacting Your Lenders

Section Three: Contacting Your Lenders

Now that you have gathered and organized all relevant information, it is time to contact your lender. **Do not be afraid of this conversation – there is more danger in silence than in regular, open communication with your mortgage company.** Although you may anticipate your lender is working against you, please remember that the lending partner benefits most by the consistent payment of your mortgage than by taking your property, so their primary goal is to get you back on track.

The first thing you should do is request your updated reinstatement and payoff figures. You may have received these figures in the mail, but updated figures are best. Some lenders require 24-36 hours to process a reinstatement or payoff request – get it as soon as possible. Order BOTH – these requests will give you up-to-date and accurate numbers and deadline dates.

The next question you should ask your lender is, "What workout solutions are you authorized and required to offer?" You should also ask, "Who is the loan mitigation authority for the lender?" You are entitled to this information. It is absolutely essential that you communicate with the right person. Speak only to an individual who is authorized to enter into and approve a workout agreement.

It is important to get the correct phone numbers, fax numbers, and addresses of your lenders and associated law firms. All communication MUST be documented – it is in your best interest to create a paper trail of evidence that proves you are attempting to resolve the situation. After speaking with your lending partner, ask for documentation that summarizes your conversation or agreement, and keep these letters in your files.

Lastly, BE PERSISTENT. If you do not get to the person you need to speak to on the first try, TRY AGAIN. Your home is at stake – be unrelenting and determined in your communication until you get the results you need.

Do not proceed to this section until you have completed everything in the previous sections.

Mortgage Company Discussion – 1st Trust

During the meeting with your mortgage company, you will be giving and receiving a great amount of information. WRITE EVERYTHING DOWN. You will need this information every time you speak with someone about your situation.

FIRST MORTGAGE:

Lender:	
Lender Phone:	
Lender Fax:	
Address:	
Account/Loan #:	
Conversation Date:	
Foreclosure Dept. Phone:	
Foreclosure Dept. Fax:	
Name of Representative:	
Rep's Extension:	
Number of Months Behind:	
Payoff Amount :	
Reinstatement Amount:	
Interest/Penalties:	

Is a loan workout/forbearance agreement available? ☐ Yes ☐ No
If yes, write details of forbearance agreement in the Discussion Points on the following page.

Has the loan been referred to a law firm? ☐ Yes ☐ No

Law Firm Name	
Law Firm Phone Number	
Law Firm File Number	

Discussion Points:

Conversation Date: _____

_____

_____

_____

_____

_____

_____

_____

_____

_____

_____

_____

_____

_____

_____

_____

_____

_____

_____

_____

_____

_____

_____

_____

_____

Mortgage Company Discussion – 2nd Trust

During the meeting with your mortgage company, you will be giving and receiving a great amount of information. WRITE EVERYTHING DOWN. You will need this information <u>every time</u> you speak with someone about your situation.

SECOND MORTGAGE:

Lender:	
Lender Phone:	
Lender Fax:	
Address:	
Account/Loan #:	
Conversation Date:	
Foreclosure Dept. Phone:	
Foreclosure Dept. Fax:	
Name of Representative:	
Rep's Extension:	
Number of Months Behind:	
Payoff Amount :	
Reinstatement Amount:	
Interest/Penalties:	

Is a loan workout/forbearance agreement available?   ☐ Yes ☐ No
If yes, write details of forbearance agreement in the Discussion Points on the following page.

Has the loan been referred to a law firm?   ☐ Yes ☐ No

Law Firm Name	
Law Firm Phone Number	
Law Firm File Number	

Discussion Points:

Conversation Date: _____

_____

_____

_____

_____

_____

_____

_____

_____

_____

_____

_____

_____

_____

_____

_____

_____

_____

_____

_____

_____

_____

_____

_____

_____

Law Firm Discussion

During the meeting with the law firm assigned to your foreclosure case, you will be giving and receiving a great amount of information. WRITE EVERYTHING DOWN. You will need this information every time you speak with someone about your situation.

Law Firm:	
Law Firm Phone:	
Law Firm Fax:	
Address:	
Account/Loan #:	
Law Firm File #:	
Name of Representative:	
Rep's Extension:	
Auction Date/Sheriff's Sale:	
Auction/Sale Location:	
Number of Months Behind:	
Payoff Amount:	
Reinstatement Amount:	
Interest/Penalties:	
Payoff Deadline Date:	
Reinstatement Deadline Date:	

Discussion Points:

Conversation Date: _____

_____
_____
_____
_____
_____
_____
_____
_____
_____
_____
_____
_____
_____
_____
_____
_____
_____
_____
_____
_____
_____
_____
_____
_____

Discussion Points:

Conversation Date: _____

_____
_____
_____
_____
_____
_____
_____
_____
_____
_____
_____
_____
_____
_____
_____
_____
_____
_____
_____
_____
_____
_____
_____
_____

**Do not proceed until the previous
worksheets are completed.**

Section Four:
What Are Your Options?

Section Four: What Are Your Options?

Now that you have gathered all the relevant information and conducted meetings with your mortgage lender and assigned law firm, it is time to review the options you have available to you. The next few worksheets will assist you in choosing the best solution for you based on your circumstances.

Do not make any final decisions until you have read all of Section Three and have weighed all the options available to you.

Do not proceed to this section until you have completed everything in the previous sections.

Option #1: Lender Payment Plans

The option of reinstating your loan is viable if you have the funds to pay back the delinquent balance in a specified time frame (less than 24 months). Your lender will comprise an agreement that breaks up the outstanding balance and adds it to your current mortgage payment amount. This means two specific things that you must be aware of:

1. Your mortgage payment <u>WILL</u> be a higher amount for a period of time.
2. You will be required to make an initial payment towards this agreement for it to go into affect.

The options you will be offered may include the following:

Full Reinstatement
If you have the funds available (or will have the funds in a short time), your loan can be reinstated in a single payment. Your lender can accept a certified check or initiate a draft from your bank account for the past due balance and assessed fees.

Partial Reinstatement – Monthly Repayment Plan
Your loan can also be reinstated by working out a monthly repayment plan. In addition to your regular loan payment, an additional partial payment can be added on to pay down your arrears. <u>Your lender will most likely ask you for a deposit for the payment agreement to be accepted</u>. Your lender can accept a certified check or initiate a draft from your bank account for the past due balance and assessed fees.

Forbearance Plan
Your loan payments can be reduced or suspended for a period of time, after which, the back payments are made up through a balloon payment or monthly repayment plan. A forbearance agreement must be approved by a lender – the required paperwork, hardship letter, and workout plan must be submitted and an agreement letter signed before a forbearance plan can take affect.

Review the information on the **Assess Your Current Situation** and **Financial Information** worksheets to see if you have the funds available to commit to a repayment plan. Remember, your payments will INCREASE. If you do not have the funds available on a monthly basis, or the upfront money required, <u>do not commit to a payment arrangement with your lender</u>.

Additional Lender Options

These are additional options that can be discussed directly with your lender. Again, read through all options before coming to a final conclusion – no one can make the right decision without first having the right knowledge!

Mortgage Modification

If your income has been unexpectedly reduced and you cannot pay the current mortgage amount, but you could pay a smaller amount, you may qualify for a mortgage modification. You may be able to refinance the debt and/or extend the term of your mortgage loan. This may help you catch up by reducing the monthly payments to a more affordable level. You will need to qualify by submitting proof of your reduced income and ability to pay a lesser loan payment.

Partial Claim

This applies to FHA mortgages only – your lender may be able to work with you to obtain a one-time payment from the FHA-Insurance fund to bring your mortgage current. You may qualify for a Partial Claim if:

- Your loan is at least 4 months delinquent but no more than 12 months delinquent;
- You are able to begin making full mortgage payments.

When your lender files a Partial Claim, the U.S. Department of Housing and Urban Development will pay your lender the amount necessary to bring your mortgage current. You must execute a Promissory Note, and a Lien will be placed on your property until the Promissory Note is paid in full. The Promissory Note is interest-free and is due when you pay off the first mortgage or when you sell the property.

Short Sale

If your house is not worth more than what you currently owe, the lender may allow a short sale. This will allow you to avoid foreclosure by selling your property on the market for an amount less than the amount necessary to pay off your mortgage loan. You may qualify for a property short sale if:

- The loan is at least 2 months delinquent;
- You are able to sell your house within 3 to 5 months; and
- A new appraisal (that your lender will obtain) shows that the value of your home is less than the mortgage amount.

A short sale is NOT a last-minute option: there is a specific process that must be followed to the letter if you are going to submit a short sale package to your lender for acceptance. Again, a short sale MUST be approved by the lender prior to selling your home. You will need to work with your lender's Loss Mitigation department to obtain the criteria for approval.

Deed-in-Lieu of Foreclosure

As a last resort, you may be able to voluntarily "give back" your property to the lender. This won't save your house, but it is not as damaging to your credit rating as a foreclosure. You can qualify for a deed-in-lieu of foreclosure if:

- You are in default and don't qualify for any of the other options;
- Your attempts at selling the house before foreclosure were unsuccessful; and
- You don't have another mortgage in default.

Some of these options are only available to you if you are still living in the home. Your lender or a qualified housing counselor (see Resources and Contacts) will determine if you qualify for any of the alternatives. Most lenders will not object to any reasonable plan, provided it does not compromise the lien position or come into conflict with any other policy or commitment.

Option #2: Angels

"Angels" are those individuals who have the financial means available, and are willing to give you the money you need, to reinstate your loan without expecting immediate or structured repayment.

Make a list of names of possible Angels in your circle. Do not forget to include family friends, church connections, and business associates.

Angels References:

1. _____

2. _____

3. _____

4. _____

5. _____

6. _____

7. _____

8. _____

9. _____

10. _____

Option #3: Loan for Arrears Amount

Lenders, unlike "Angels", provide you with a loan and expect repayment, often with terms added.

When you arrange a loan for the amount you need, be sure to specify your exit strategy, such as:

- length of loan
- possible interest
- monthly payments or a balloon payment at the end of the term
- penalties for non-payment

Based on you current financial situation, what are you prepared to propose as a repayment plan?

Amount needed:

_____

Least acceptable amount required:

_____

Months to repay:

_____

Interest rate:

_____

Balloon or monthly payment:

_____

Non-payment penalty:

_____

If you are borrowing from multiple lenders, review the information on the **Assess Your Current Situation** and **Financial Information** worksheets and consider how the combined payments, interests, and fees will impact your short and long term cash flow plan.

Make a list of names of possible Loan Providers in your circle. Do not forget to include family friends, church connections, and business associates. Look to online loan resources, such as Prosper.com.

Loan Provider References:

1. _____

2. _____

3. _____

4. _____

5. _____

6. _____

7. _____

8. _____

9. _____

10. _____

Option #4: Refinance/Debt Consolidation

A mortgage refinance or debt consolidation loan for a preforeclosure property is difficult, but not impossible. If you have a good amount of equity in your home, your chances of being able to refinance are improved.

Be prepared to pay a much higher interest rate, upfront appraisal fees, and to come up with money for closing costs.

The necessary factors for refinance are:
- Credit Score
- Income
- Home Equity
- Job History
- Monthly Expenses
- Current Debt
- Cash for Closing
- Appraisal Fees

To find a refinance program, first ask for referrals from friends, family, and associates. Then, research advertisements for debt consolidation or mortgage refinance in your local newspaper (Real Estate section). When you contact the agencies, ask the following questions:

1. Are you a mortgage broker or a direct lender?
2. Do you work with problem credit/preforeclosure properties?
3. What is the lowest FICO (credit) score you accept for refinancing?
4. How much equity is required for your refinancing program?
5. How long is your approval and funding process (you will need this information to determine if they will work quickly enough to stop a foreclosure)?
6. What are the fees involved?
7. What is the proposed interest rate?
8. Is the interest rate fixed or adjustable?

Use the worksheets on the following pages to record the details of your conversations. Then review the information on the **Assess Your Current Situation** and **Financial Information** worksheets to see if the proposed payments are feasible within your monthly budget.

Refinance/Debt Consolidation – Agency #1

Conversation Date: _____

Mortgage broker or direct lender?   ☐ Broker   ☐ Lender

Preforeclosure programs?   ☐ Yes   ☐ No

Lowest FICO score accepted: _____

Amount of equity required: _____

Length of approval/funding process: _____

Fees: _____

Proposed monthly payment: _____

Proposed interest rate: _____

Fixed or adjustable: ☐ Fixed   ☐ ARM

Additional Discussion Points:

_____

_____

_____

_____

_____

_____

_____

_____

_____

_____

_____

_____

Refinance/Debt Consolidation – Agency #2

Conversation Date: _____

Mortgage broker or direct lender?	☐ Broker ☐ Lender
Preforeclosure programs?	☐ Yes ☐ No
Lowest FICO score accepted:	_____
Amount of equity required:	_____
Length of approval/funding process:	_____
Fees:	_____
Proposed monthly payment:	_____
Proposed interest rate:	_____
Fixed or adjustable:	☐ Fixed ☐ ARM

Additional Discussion Points:

_____

_____

_____

_____

_____

_____

_____

_____

_____

_____

_____

Refinance/Debt Consolidation – Agency #3

Conversation Date: _____

Mortgage broker or direct lender?	☐ Broker ☐ Lender
Preforeclosure programs?	☐ Yes ☐ No
Lowest FICO score accepted:	_____
Amount of equity required:	_____
Length of approval/funding process:	_____
Fees:	_____
Proposed monthly payment:	_____
Proposed interest rate:	_____
Fixed or adjustable:	☐ Fixed ☐ ARM

Additional Discussion Points:

_____

_____

_____

_____

_____

_____

_____

_____

_____

_____

_____

Option #5: Loss Mitigation

Loss Mitigation firms promote "Mortgage Assistance Programs" that are specifically designed to stop foreclosure and help people who are behind in their mortgage payments keep their homes, while they get back on track with their payments. Essentially, you are paying a firm to initiate Option #1 for you.

A Loss Mitigation firm typically provides a free consultation to assess your situation, and then ask for a deposit before working on your case. Their fees are usually combined with the workout agreement with the mortgage companies.

To find a qualified Loss Mitigation firm, obtain a reference from a HUD-approved housing counselor by calling 800-569-4287 (800-877-8339 for the hearing impaired).

Loss Mitigation References:

Reference #1

Firm:

Representative:

Phone & Fax:

Email:

Website:

Reference #2

Firm:

Representative:

Phone & Fax:

Email:

Website:

Reference #3

Firm:

Representative:

Phone & Fax:

Email:

Website:

When contacting a Loss Mitigation firm, you will need to reference the information you have obtained regarding your financial situation, your mortgage details, and specifics about your foreclosure case.

Option #6: Property Sale with Realtor

Before you undertake the process of selling your home, be sure that you communicate with your Lender and let them know you are putting the house up for sale. They may ask for verification of this action, such as a Realtor agreement and a copy of the listing on the Multiple Listing Service. In order to stop a foreclosure on a property, you will need an official contract for sale and a letter from a lending institution that states they are funding the deal. A "pre-approval" letter from a lender or mortgage broker is not acceptable.

If you choose to sell your home to avoid foreclosure, using a Realtor to assist you can be beneficial. A Realtor is qualified to give you information on the housing prices in your area, the number of days a house stays on the market before sale in your neighborhood, and the steps you need to take to prepare your house to sell. This information is critical to assessing if you have enough time to sell your home to the public.

A Realtor's fee can be as high as 6% of the purchase price, so you will need to ensure that the housing sale price covers the following:

- Mortgage Payoff
- Realtor Fees
- Taxes and Transfer Costs
- Any Property or IRS Liens or Judgments

To find a Realtor, first ask for referrals from friends, family, and associates. You may have already received postcards or correspondence from Realtors in your area, so it is likely they would be willing to work or have worked with preforeclosure properties.

Realtor References:

Reference #1

Realtor Name/Firm: _____

Phone: _____

Email: _____

Reference #2

Realtor Name/Firm: _____

Phone: _____

Email: _____

Reference #3

Realtor Name/Firm: _____

Phone: _____

Email: _____

The "For Sale By Owner" Option

If you are interested in selling your home, but do not want to use the services of a Realtor, you can sell your home on your own. Your house would then be listed as For Sale by Owner (FSBO). There are pros and cons to selling your house yourself:

PROS:
Selling your home without an agent means more money in your pocket. By selling it yourself you save the fees or commissions (thousands of dollars) that you would have to pay an agent.

You are able to decide the times for open houses and showings as well as where you want to advertise. Because you are only selling one home - unlike an agent who is working with many buyers and sellers - you will always be focused on the selling of your home. You will have more interest in the sale than a real estate agent who may be looking for bigger commissions elsewhere.

CONS:
The For Sale by Owner option only works if you are not facing IMMEDIATE foreclosure. Again, in order to stop a foreclosure on a property, you will need an official contract for sale and a letter from a lending institution that states they are funding the deal. A "pre-approval" letter from a lender or mortgage broker is not acceptable.

Selling a home takes a lot of time and energy. Open houses, dealing with potential buyers, closing sales and dealing with the legal issues are familiar turf for Realtors, and their experience can impact the sale.

For FSBO assistance, research the following websites:

- www.forsalebyowner.com
- www.fsbo.com
- www.helpusell.com

Option #7: Investor Sale

For a quicker sale, you may want to look into selling your house to a Real Estate Investor. An investor's only focus is purchasing houses – usually in "as-is" condition, and always at a significantly lower amount than market price. Working with an investor can be a quick process, as they usually are able to many factors that need to be reviewed before a purchase is made.

An Investor considers the following factors:

- Condition of the house (interior and exterior)
- Fix-up/Repair costs
- Cash needed (purchase and closing costs)
- Title Inspection
- Transfer and Recordation fees
- Title insurance
- Appraisal fees
- Arrears
- Mortgage Payoff
- Carrying costs (including insurance, utilities, taxes)
- Market conditions
- Neighborhood condition
- Comparable sales

An investor is ALWAYS looking to buy your house at a discount – at least 70% of the market value price, or the after-repair value of your property. For example, if your house is valued at $100,000 after it has been repaired, an investor will want to purchase your house for $70,000. You will need to assess whether this equation will provide you with enough to pay off your house and satisfy your financial requirements. For caution's sake, you should calculate how much an offer will be at a 25%, 30%, and 35% discount.

			x 65%	=	
Market Value	minus	Repairs			Investor Price

			x 70%	=	
Market Value	minus	Repairs			Investor Price

			x 75%	=	
Market Value	minus	Repairs			Investor Price

Foreclosure Consultants
In some states, it's the LAW!

Many homeowners facing foreclosure may decide to sell their homes to an investor. Unfortunately, investors have not always been "above board" in their dealings with homeowners, and several property holders have found themselves holding empty promises and bad debts while the investor walks away with the property.

With all the recent foreclosure activity throughout the nation, several states have enacted laws to protect the homeowner from making an uninformed decision about their home. In the last two years, Michigan, Maryland, Colorado, and Illinois have created strict laws that purchasers must adhere to, and have created the role of Foreclosure Consultant to provide information and assist the property holder in making an educated choice about their home.

In the states that have strict laws against an Investor contacting you directly to purchase your home, you will need to work with a middleman to sell your home to an Investor. The role of the middleman is to clearly explain your options and rights when you are facing foreclosure. A lawyer, real estate agent or broker, or Foreclosure Consultant are some examples of legally-defined "middlemen", and can assist you with your property sale. These professions are performing a service for a fee, and <u>do not</u> have an equitable interest in the sale of your home.

To explain this clearly, you should understand the differences between a Foreclosure Consultant and a Foreclosure Purchaser (an Investor).

A **Foreclosure Consultant** is a person who makes a solicitation, representation, or offer to a homeowner at risk of foreclosure to perform, or who performs, one of a number of specified services that the person represents will help the homeowner. (Definition from MD Bill SB761)

A Foreclosure Consultant CANNOT:

- Buy a pre-foreclosure property.
- Have an equitable interest in the sale of the property.
- Induce the homeowner to sign documentation that waives their rights regarding the transfer of ownership of their property.
- Have "agency" with one investor/investment firm.

A **Foreclosure Purchaser** (Investor) is a person who acquires title or possession of a deed or other document to a residence in foreclosure. **

A Foreclosure Purchaser CANNOT:

- Market directly to homeowners in pre-foreclosure.
- Have initial contact homeowners to discuss options.
- Negotiate directly with mortgage companies and law firms on behalf of the property owner.
- Induce the homeowner to sign documentation that waives their rights regarding the transfer of ownership of their property.

A Foreclosure Consultant and a Foreclosure Purchaser are <u>two separate entities</u>. One person cannot be both. If a person represents him/herself as a Foreclosure Consultant and offers to purchase your home, they may not be working in the utmost integrity.

If you are selling the house yourself to avoid foreclosure, check to see if there are any complaints against the prospective buyer. You can contact your state's Attorney General, the State Real Estate Commission, or the local District Attorney's Consumer Fraud Unit for this type of information.

Here are the states (as of the date of publication) that have enacted laws to protect homeowners from foreclosure scams:

Michigan	Minnesota	Maryland
Illinois	Colorado	California
Georgia	Missouri	New York
Rhode Island	Washington	Florida

Other states (such as the District of Columbia) have introduced bills similar to the ones above. If your state has not yet considered a bill such as these, call your legislator. This is a VERY public issue... they will listen!

Investor References:

Reference #1

Investor Name/Firm: _____

Phone: _____

Email: _____

Website: _____

Reference #2

Investor Name/Firm: _____

Phone: _____

Email: _____

Website: _____

Reference #3

Investor Name/Firm: _____

Phone: _____

Email: _____

Website: _____

Foreclosure Consultant References:

Reference #1

Consultant Name/Firm: _____

Phone: _____

Email: _____

Website: _____

Reference #2

Consultant Name/Firm: _____

Phone: _____

Email: _____

Website: _____

Reference #3

Consultant Name/Firm: _____

Phone: _____

Email: _____

Website: _____

Option #8: Bankruptcy

Bankruptcy is a federal court process designed to help consumers and businesses eliminate their debts or repay them under the protection of the bankruptcy court. Bankruptcies can generally be described as "liquidation" or "reorganization."

Chapter 7 Bankruptcy: Under a liquidation bankruptcy, you ask the bankruptcy court to wipe out (discharge) the debts you owe. In exchange for this discharge, the bankruptcy trustee can take any property you own that is not exempt from collection, sell it, and distribute the proceeds to your creditors.

Chapter 13 Bankruptcy: Under a reorganization bankruptcy, you file a plan with the bankruptcy court proposing how you will repay your creditors. You must use your income to pay some or all of what you owe to your creditors over time – from three to five years, depending on the size of your debts and income.

Before you can file for bankruptcy, you MUST receive credit counseling from an agency approved by the United States Trustee's office (see the Resources and Contacts section). These agencies are allowed to charge a fee for their services, but if you cannot afford to pay, they must provide counseling for free or at reduced rates. Once you've completed your counseling, the credit counseling agency will give you a certificate showing that you met the requirement.

To begin your bankruptcy case, you must file this certificate with the bankruptcy court, along with a packet of forms listing what you own, earn, owe, and spend. You'll also need to submit your federal tax return for the previous year and proof that you filed federal and state tax returns for the previous four years. In addition, you must file a Chapter 13 repayment plan showing how you will pay off your debt and pay the filing fee.

Bankruptcy is not a definite solution. The American Bar Association has reported that 96% of homeowners who declare bankruptcy end up losing their home to foreclosure anyway. If you do not make timely payments and strictly adhere to the rules, the bankruptcy WILL be cancelled and the foreclosure process will be reinstated immediately. If you decide to declare bankruptcy, you WILL need a competent attorney to assist you in choosing the right bankruptcy filing for your situation, gathering all the required information, and filing the correct paperwork and adhering to the court imposed timeline.

Bankruptcy Attorney References:

Reference #1

Attorney Name: _____

Firm: _____

Phone: _____

Email: _____

Website: _____

Reference #2

Attorney Name: _____

Firm: _____

Phone: _____

Email: _____

Website: _____

Reference #3

Attorney Name: _____

Firm: _____

Phone: _____

Email: _____

Website: _____

Option #9: Doing Nothing

Although it is necessary to mention this as an option, because it is an option that some choose, it is not one that we recommend in any way, shape, or form.

This is the worst possible decision. If you do nothing about your situation, you WILL lose your home. Your property will be foreclosed upon and sold at auction. Your credit will be ruined and you will lose the equity in your home. After foreclosure, it is difficult to get a loan on another property.

Consequences of Foreclosure

Foreclosure is extremely damaging to your credit rating and financial future. Some of the consequences are:

- **Loss of property** – you WILL lose your property if the foreclosure process goes through the complete cycle. The property will be sold at auction or repossessed by the bank.

- **Damaged credit rating** – a foreclosure is worse on your credit rating than a Bankruptcy; it says to a credit lender that you made no attempt to fix your situation! You will need to be prepared to pay cash or high interest rates for anything that requires credit – an immediate apartment, a future house, car, even a cell phone.

- **Possible loss of employment** – if you have a job that requires a security clearance or a responsible financial background, a foreclosure is detrimental to your employment.

- **Possible deficiency judgment** – if the house is sold at auction for less than is owed, you are then responsible for the monetary difference. So, even though the house is no longer in your possession, the lender can still come after you by filing a deficiency judgment for the amount that was not collected.

Additional Notes

_____

_____

_____

_____

_____

_____

_____

_____

_____

_____

_____

_____

_____

_____

_____

_____

_____

_____

_____

_____

_____

_____

_____

_____

_____

Additional Notes

Section Five:
Choosing Your Options and Taking Action!

Section Five: Choosing Your Options and Taking Action!

Congratulations! You have accurately reviewed your personal and financial situation, conducted meetings with your lender and assigned law firm, and have reviewed the options that you have available to you. Based on the information you have gathered, it is now time to make the final decision on the options you will choose and take action!

It is always a good idea to implement more than one option at a time – this way, as your timeline is getting shorter, you are able to have more than one solution working for you.

Which Option(s) have you chosen to pursue?

- ☐ Option 1: Lender Repayment Plan/Additional Lender Options
- ☐ Option 2: Angels
- ☐ Option 3: Loan for Arrears
- ☐ Option 4: Refinance/Debt Consolidation
- ☐ Option 5: Loss Mitigation
- ☐ Option 6: Sale with Realtor/FSBO
- ☐ Option 7: Sale with Investor
- ☐ Option 8: Bankruptcy
- ☐ Option 9: Doing Nothing

Why have you chosen the option(s) that you have?

_____

_____

_____

_____

_____

_____

_____

_____

So, Now That I'm Finished, What's Next?

Now that you have reviewed your options and are taking steps to rectify your financial situation, you should take two additional steps to turn your financial stumbling blocks into prosperity stepping stones once and for all:

1. Sign up with a Credit Repair Service.

No matter what stage your foreclosure is in, if you are late on your house payments, your credit is affected. Poor credit can wreak havoc on your financial future – it greatly impacts how much you pay for anything, including car and credit card financing. You MUST think of your future, and taking the step to sign up for a credit counseling service will assist you getting your finances back on track.

Here's how you start:

a. Order your FICO scores from **www.myfico.com**. You cannot get your FICO scores for free, so do not get generic credit scores from one of the many websites that offers them for free. You must get FICO (Fair Isaac Corporation) scores. And you must get all three of your FICO credit scores (one from each of the credit reporting agencies).

b. On each one of your credit scores, look for your negative reason codes. Each FICO score will have four negative reason codes listed. These negative reason codes tell you EXACTLY what you need to do to increase your credit scores. They are listed in the order of importance. So, start by fixing the top reason code for each score.

c. Hire a law firm to help you dispute inaccurate, incomplete, misleading or unverifiable items on your credit reports. There's only so much you can do by yourself. Having a law firm that specializes in dealing with credit can help you in your quest to improve your credit quicker than you would be able to on your own. We recommend **Lexington Law Firm (www.lexingtonlaw.com)** – affordable prices, monthly payment plans, and great results.

2. Read our Living Paycheck-to-Prosperous™ Blog!
Our blog will provide prosperity tips, better living resources, and advice on financial subjects ranging from budgeting to the best books to read. This is a must read! Visit us at **lp2p.blogspot.com**!

Additional Notes

_____

_____

_____

_____

_____

_____

_____

_____

_____

_____

_____

_____

_____

_____

_____

_____

_____

_____

_____

_____

_____

_____

_____

_____

_____

_____

_____

Resources & Contacts

Government Agencies

U.S. Department of Housing and Urban Development (HUD)
Main Office
451 7th Street SW
Washington, DC 20410
202-708-1112
202-708-1455 (TTY)
www.hud.gov
Contact the main number or visit the website to locate an office in your area.

Internal Revenue Service (IRS)
1-800-829-1040
1-800-829-4059 (TDD)
www.irs.gov
Contact the main number or visit the website to locate an office in your area.

Credit and Financial Counseling

Mandatory Bankruptcy Counseling:	For a list of approved agencies, go to the Trustee's website at: **www.usdoj.gov/ust** Click Credit Counseling and Debtor Education
VA Foreclosure Counseling:	VA Regional Loan Centers have technicians available to conduct financial counseling to help you avoid foreclosure. Call **1-800-827-1000** or visit **www.homeloans.va.gov/paytrbl.htm**
Foreclosure Counseling:	For a nearby HUD approved counseling agency, call **1-800-569-4287** or **1-800-877-8339 (TDD)**. Fannie Mae offers home ownership counseling services to assist delinquent borrowers in managing debt. For the home-buyer education specialist in your area call **1-800-7FANNIE**.

Credit Agencies

Equifax
P.O. Box 740241
Atlanta, GA 30374
1-800-685-1111
www.Equifax.com

Experian
P.O. Box 2002
Allen, TX 75013
1-888-397-3742
www.Experian.com

Trans Union
P.O. Box 1000
Chester, PA 19022
1-800-888-4213
www.Transunion.com

FICO Scores
www.myfico.com – a division of Fair Isaac Corporation (FICO)
1-800-319-4433

How to Request Your Free Credit Report

To comply with the FACTA legislation, the three major credit bureaus have jointly set up a website so that the public can order their free credit reports over the Internet. The website is **www.annualcreditreport.com**. You can also request your free credit reports by calling or by writing to:

Annual Credit Request Service
P. O. Box 105281
Atlanta, GA 30348-5281
1-877-322-8228

Procedures by State

This is a general guide only – it is common for laws to change, so you will to check your state statutes for accurate, up to date procedures. A review of the following table:

- **Type of Foreclosure** – Judicial, Non-Judicial, or Both
- **Months to Foreclose** – the legal minimum required and the probable time length once foreclosure has begun.
- **Deficiency Judgments** – the states in which deficiency judgments are available if the lender loses money through the foreclosure process, and if it is or is not practical for the lender to enforce a judgment.
- **Redemption Period** – which states have redemption periods and the time frame, where available.

STATE	TYPE OF FORECLOSURE	MONTHS TO FORECLOSE MINIMUM/EXPECTED	DEFICIENCY JUDGMENT	REDEMPTION PERIOD
Alabama	Primarily Non-Judicial	1/3	Possible and Practical	12 Months
Alaska	Both	3/4	Not Practical	None
Arizona	Both	3/4	Not Practical	None
Arkansas	Both	4/5	Possible and Practical	None
California	Primarily Non-Judicial	4/4	Not Practical	None
Colorado	Both	2/5	Possible and Practical	75 Days

STATE	TYPE OF FORECLOSURE	MONTHS TO FORECLOSE MINIMUM/EXPECTED	DEFICIENCY JUDGMENT	REDEMPTION PERIOD
Connecticut	Judicial/Strict	5/6	Possible and Practical	None
Delaware	Judicial	3/7	Possible and Practical	None
District of Columbia	Non-Judicial	2/4	Possible and Practical	None
Florida	Judicial	5/5	Possible and Practical	None
Georgia	Primarily Non-Judicial	2/2	Possible and Practical	None
Hawaii	Primarily Non-Judicial	3/4	Not Practical	None
Idaho	Non-Judicial	5/6	Possible and Practical	None
Illinois	Judicial	7/10	Possible and Practical	None
Indiana	Judicial	5/7	Possible and Practical	3 Months
Iowa	Both	5/6	Not Practical	6 Months, if judicial
Kansas	Judicial	4/4	Possible and Practical	6-12 Months
Kentucky	Judicial	6/5	Possible and Practical	None
Louisiana	Judicial	2/6	Possible and Practical	None
Maine	Primarily Judicial	6/10	Possible and Practical	None
Maryland	Judicial	2/2	Possible and Practical	None

STATE	TYPE OF FORECLOSURE	MONTHS TO FORECLOSE MINIMUM/EXPECTED	DEFICIENCY JUDGMENT	REDEMPTION PERIOD
Massachusetts	Non-Judicial	3/4	Possible and Practical	None
Michigan	Both	2/2	Possible and Practical	6 Months
Minnesota	Both	2/3	Not Practical	6 Months
Mississippi	Primarily Non-Judicial	2/3	Possible and Practical	None
Missouri	Primarily Non-Judicial	2/2	Possible and Practical	None
Montana	Primarily Non-Judicial	5/5	Not Practical	None
Nebraska	Judicial	5/6	Possible and Practical	None
Nevada	Primarily Non-Judicial	4/4	Possible and Practical	None
New Hampshire	Primarily Non-Judicial	2/3	Possible and Practical	None
New Jersey	Judicial	3/10	Possible and Practical	10 Days
New Mexico	Judicial	4/6	Possible and Practical	None
New York	Judicial	4/8	Possible and Practical	None
North Carolina	Non-Judicial	2/4	Possible and Practical	None
North Dakota	Judicial	3/5	Not Possible	60 Days
Ohio	Judicial	5/7	Possible and Practical	None

STATE	TYPE OF FORECLOSURE	MONTHS TO FORECLOSE MINIMUM/EXPECTED	DEFICIENCY JUDGMENT	REDEMPTION PERIOD
Oklahoma	Primarily Judicial	4/7	Possible and Practical	None
Oregon	Non-Judicial	5/5	Not Practical	None
Pennsylvania	Judicial	3/9	Not Practical	None
Rhode Island	Both	2/3	Possible and Practical	None
South Carolina	Judicial	6/6	Not Practical	None
Tennessee	Non-Judicial	2/2	Possible and Practical	None
Texas	Non-Judicial	2/2	Possible and Practical	None
Utah	Both	4/5	Possible and Practical	None
Vermont	Both	7/10	Possible and Practical	None
Virginia	Non-Judicial	2/2	Possible and Practical	None
Washington	Non-Judicial	4/5	Not Practical	None
West Virginia	Non-Judicial	2/2	Possible and Practical	None
Wisconsin	Judicial	varies/10	Not Practical	None
Wyoming	Non-Judicial	2/3	Possible and Practical	3 Months

Foreclosure Glossary

This glossary will assist you in defining commonly used foreclosure terminology.

Abandonment	A process in bankruptcy wherein the court releases a property from its control when it is deemed to have no value to the estate.
Abstract	A succinct summary; (e.g. an abstract of judgment; an abstract of title, etc.)
Abstract of Judgment	The essentials of a money judgment obtained via an adjudicated lawsuit. When an abstract is recorded in the recorder's office, the judgment becomes a general lien on the entire debtor's property located in that particular county.
Acceleration Clause	Clause in a deed of trust or mortgage which "accelerates" the time when the indebtedness becomes due. For example, some mortgages or deeds of trust contain a provision that the note balance shall become due immediately upon the resale of the land or upon the default in the payment of principal and interest.
Acknowledgment	A formal declaration before a duly authorized officer (such as a notary public) by a person who has executed an instrument that such execution is his own. An acknowledgment is necessary to entitle an instrument (with certain specific exceptions) to be recorded, to impart constructive notice of its contents, and to entitle the instrument to be used as evidence without further proof. The certificate of acknowledgment is attached to the instrument or incorporated therein.
Acquisition	An act or process, such as foreclosure, by which one procures ownership of property.
Addendum	An addition or change to a contract.
Adjudication	A judicial determination.
Adjustable Rate Mortgage (ARM)	A loan with an interest rate that fluctuates based on a specified financial index.

Administrator	If a person dies without a Will (Intestate), the Court will appoint a person, or Administrator, to handle the Estate, whose functions are similar to those of an Executor
Ad Valorem Tax	A tax based on the value of the property as a percentage of that value.
Advances	Moneys paid, on behalf of an owner, by a junior interest holder. Done to temporarily cure a delinquency on a senior encumbrance that threatens to extinguish the junior's position. Thereafter the junior lien holder can start their own foreclosure if they are not immediately reimbursed for the advances paid out.
Adverse Possession	A means of acquiring title where an occupant has been in actual, open, notorious, and continuous occupancy of a property under a claim of right for the required statutory period.
Affidavit	A sworn, notarized statement that's signed by the affiant before witnesses.
Agency	The relationship of trust that exists between sellers and buyers and their real estate agents. The agency is formed through a written contract.
Agent	A person licensed by the state to conduct real estate transactions.
Agreement of Sale	A signed, written contract entered into between the seller and buyer for sale of real property under certain specific terms and conditions.
Alienation	The transfer of an interest in or title to property to another.
Amortization	The gradual repayment of a debt in a series of equal periodic amounts until the total debt, including interest, is paid in full. Senior loans are typically amortized over 30 years, whereas junior loans are generally amortized over a much shorter time period.

Appraisal	A statement of value or estimation of the value of a property as of a certain date conducted by a disinterested person with suitable qualifications. Generally, value for single family properties is based upon a review of recent market activity using sales of comparable properties as a basis and then making value adjustments based upon the comparison of comparable property to the subject property.
Appreciation	Increase in value or worth. The difference between the increased value of property and the original sales price.
Annual Percentage Rate (APR)	The cost of the loan expressed as a yearly rate on the balance of the loan.
Anticipatory Breach	A communication that informs a party that the obligations of the original contract will not be fulfilled.
Appurtenance	A right, privilege, or improvement belonging to, or passing with, the land.
Arm's Length Transaction	A transaction between relative strangers, each trying to do the best for himself, or herself.
As-Is Condition	The purchase or sale of a property in its existing condition
Assessment	A bonded tax imposed to pay for public improvements (e.g. street/alley paving, curbs, sidewalks, etc.) beneficial to a limited area . Paid semiannually over a 10 year period to the Bond Division of the city or county treasurer's office where the property is located.
Assessed Value	Assessed Value applies in ad valorem taxation and refers to the value of a property according to tax roles. Assessed value may not conform to market value, but it is usually calculated to a market value base. A tax assessor's determination of the value of a home in order to calculate a tax base.
Assignee	One to whom a transfer of an interest is made (i.e. assignee of a deed of trust).
Assignor	One who transfers property by assignment.

Assignment	Written document by which property, other than real property, is transferred from one person to another. Assignment of mortgage, assignment of deed of trust, assignment of lease, assignment of rentals, etc. are common assignments. The "assignee" receives the property assigned.
Assumption Clause	A provision that allows a buyer to take responsibility for the mortgage from a seller.
Assumption of Mortgage	A formal agreement with a lender in which a new property owner agrees to be personally liable for the repayment of a preexisting lien. Generally entails paying the lender an assumption fee and sometimes a higher interest rate.
Automatic Stay	A prevention of continuation of creditor collection activity, obtained by filing bankruptcy. Mortgagees may petition the Court to "lift" the stay and permission to resume collection activity.
Backup Offer	A secondary bid for a property that the seller will accept if the first offer fails.
Balloon Payment	A lump sum final installment payment of a promissory note that is much larger than the regular installment payments.
Bankrupt	A person who is insolvent; one whose total property is legally declared insufficient to pay his/her debts.
Bankruptcy	A proceeding in U.S. District Court wherein debtors who can not meet the claims of their creditors may be adjudged bankrupt by the court. See **Chapter 7 Bankruptcy** and **Chapter 13 Bankruptcy**.
"Bare Bones" Petition	Initial, tentative filing of a bankruptcy petition that qualifies the petitioner to the benefits of the automatic stay pending the filing of the full petition within the following 15 days. Failure to complete the filing of the full petition will result in the dismissal of the "face sheet filing" and a bar to any subsequent re-filing for the next 180 days.
Breach of Contract	The failure to perform provisions of a contract without a legal excuse.
Broker	A person licensed by the state to work in a specific field including real estate, mortgage loans, insurance, securities, etc.

Broker Price Opinion (BPO)	A written estimate of the most probable sales price of a property provided by a licensed real estate broker with experience in the specific locality of the subject property. Value of the subject property is estimated by comparing like properties that recently sold and adjusting for differences. Often provided as a means to establish a listing price for a property.
Buy Down	An upfront payment to a lender to reduce a loan's interest rate, either temporarily (the first year or two) or permanently
Buyers' Broker	A real estate broker who exclusively represents the buyer's interests in a transaction and whose commission is paid by the buyer rather than the seller.
Buyer's Market	A market with a lot fewer buyers than there are sellers, usually indicated by a prolonged marketing time of more than 90 days.
Cancellation Clause	A clause that details the conditions under which each party may terminate the agreement.
Cap	A negotiated upper limit the interest rate on a variable rate mortgage can rise, both annually and over the life of the mortgage.
Capitalization	Capitalization occurs when items owed on a loan are treated as part of a new, principal balance. When *arrears* are capitalized, the amount of the arrears is included in the principal before the interest is applied. Also a mathematical process for estimating the value of a property using a proper rate of return on the investment and annual net income expected to be produced by the property. [Income ÷ Rate = Value]
Capital Gains	Profits an investor makes from the sale of real estate or investments.
Capital Gains Tax	A tax placed on the profits from the sale of real estate or investments.
Cash Flow	The surplus left over out of the rents after paying out all operating expenses and mortgage payments.
Certificate of Reasonable Value (CRV)	An appraisal issued by the VA approved appraiser which establishes the property's current market value.

Chapter 7 Bankruptcy	Under a liquidation bankruptcy, you ask the bankruptcy court to wipe out (discharge) the debts you owe. In exchange for this discharge, the bankruptcy trustee can take any property you own that is not exempt from collection, sell it, and distribute the proceeds to your creditors.
Chapter 13 Bankruptcy	Under a reorganization bankruptcy, you file a plan with the bankruptcy court proposing how you will repay your creditors. You must use your income to pay some or all of what you owe to your creditors over time – from three to five years, depending on the size of your debts and income.
Charge Off	The process of writing off sums that have been deemed uncollectible.
Chronic Delinquent	A payment pattern wherein the borrower habitually violates the terms of the note by paying late.
Clear Title	Title that is not encumbered or burdened with defects.
Closing	The final procedure in which documents are signed and recorded, and the property is transferred.
Closing Costs	The miscellaneous costs that the buyer and seller incur to complete or "close" a real estate transaction. These costs are in addition to the price of the property - expenses incidental to the sale of real estate, including loan, title and appraisal fees. The agreement of sale negotiated previously between the buyer and the seller may state in writing who will pay each of the above costs.
Closing Statement	A document which details the final financial settlement between a buyer and seller and the costs paid by each party.
Clouded Title	Any claim, encumbrance or defect that contradicts the title record as understood by the property owner. Intractable disputes are resolved judicially.
Code	A collection of laws relating to a certain topic, such as real property, patents, etc.
Collateral	Anything of value, like real property, pledged as security for a debt.

Commission	A fee paid to a real estate agent/broker by a principal as compensation for finding a buyer or seller and completing the sale.
Commitment	A promise or firm agreement; a lender's contractual obligation to make a loan to a qualified borrower
Community Property	Some state's laws provide that where a couple acquires any asset during marriage, the husband and wife will be considered to have one-half interest in the property.
Comparables (Comps)	Similar properties that are currently listed for sale or have recently sold.
Comparable Market Analysis (CMA)	A study, intended to assist an owner in establishing a listing price, of recent, comparable sales, properties that failed to sell, and property presently on the market.
Complaint	A document commencing a lawsuit.
Compromise Sale	A VA approved short sale.
Conditional Commitment	A promise by a lender to make a loan if the borrower meets certain conditions.
Confirmation Hearing (Bankruptcy)	A hearing where the Debtors proposed Chapter 13 plan is reviewed and either approved or denied by the bankruptcy judge.
Confirmation Hearing (Foreclosure)	A hearing held subsequent to the Sheriff's Sale to confirm the sale and transfer title to the successful bidder.
Contingency	A condition specified in a purchase contract, such as the perspective buyer making an offer contingent on his or her sale of a present home, or such as a satisfactory home inspection.
Contract	An agreement entered into by two or more legally competent parties by the terms of which one or more of the parties, for a consideration, undertakes to do or refrain from doing some legal act, or acts. Essential elements of a valid contract are parties competent to contract, a proper subject matter, consideration, mutuality of agreement, and mutuality of obligation.

Contract for Deed   A contract for the sale of real estate wherein the purchase price is paid in periodic installments by the Purchaser, who is in possession of the property even though title is retained by the seller until the final payment. Also called an installment contract, or a land contract.

Contract to Purchase   A contract the buyer initiates which details the purchase price and conditions of the transaction and is accepted by the seller. Also known as an Agreement of Sale.

Conventional Mortgage   A mortgage loan not insured by HUD or guaranteed by the Veterans' Administration. It is subject to conditions established by the lending institution and State statutes.

Conversion (Bankruptcy)   The change to a case under a chapter different that the one originally filed under. The court may convert a case on the request of the debtor or the request of a party in interest.

Cosign   Agreeing to be responsible for someone else's debt.

Cramdown   A controversial procedure in bankruptcy wherein the court reduces a secured debt (i.e. trust deed or mortgage) to the current value of the property. The court actually splits the mortgage debt into two parts. The amount equal to the current value of the home is treated as a secured claim that the debtor must continue to pay. The portion of debt in excess of the property's current value becomes an unsecured claim that's usually not repaid in full.

Credit   The money a lender extends to a buyer for a commitment to repay the loan within a certain time frame.

Credit Bureau   A company that receives information about a consumer's credit history, and keeps records that are available to others seeking information on that consumer.

Credit History   A record of an individual's current and past debt payments.

Credit Rating   The degree of credit worthiness assigned to a person based on credit history and financial status.

Credit Report   A credit bureau report that shows a loan applicant's history of payments made on previous debts.

Cure a Default	With respect to delinquent mortgage loans, all missed payments have been made and loan payments are current.
Days on the Market (DOM)	The period of time a property is listed for sale until it is sold or taken off the market.
Debt Collector	The term 'debt collector' applies to collection agencies and lawyers that are collecting debt for others.
Debtor's Examination	This is normally a court ordered proceeding in which a debtor must answer questions about current income and assets from which a judgment may be collected.
Decree	A judgment by court.
Deed	A written document that transfers ownership of land from one party to another. The seller is called the "grantor" and the buyer is called the "grantee".
Deed-in-Lieu of Foreclosure	Used by owners to voluntarily convey the title of their property to the mortgagee/beneficiary (lender) to avoid the negative credit consequences of a foreclosure. Lenders are generally reluctant to accept a "deed in lieu" unless the title is free and clear of any other encumbrances junior to theirs and the owners execute an estoppel affidavit acknowledging that they are acting volitionally, with informed consent.
Default	Failure to make the loan payments as agreed in the promissory note.
Default Judgment	A judgment in a lawsuit against a defendant who did not meet the legal requirements in connection with the case.
Defendant	In a lawsuit, the person(s) or business(s) being sued.
Deferred Interest	When the amount of interest a borrower is required to pay on a mortgage loan is less than the amount of interest accrued on the outstanding principal balance. This amount is usually added to the outstanding principal balance of the mortgage loan.
Deferred Maintenance	Any repair or maintenance of a piece of property that has been postponed, resulting in a decline in property value.

Deficiency	The amount a debtor owes a creditor on a debt after the creditor seizes and sells the collateral. A deficiency arises when the collateral is sold for less than the amount of the debt.
Deficiency Judgment	A personal judgment against a debtor for the amount remaining due after a judicial foreclosure of a mortgage or a trust deed.
Delinquency	A loan payment that is at least 30 days past due. Usually after 90 days delinquency, the lender has the right to initiate foreclosure proceedings against the loan which is in default.
Delinquent Mortgage	A mortgage that involves a borrower who is behind on payments. If the borrower cannot bring the payments up to date within a specified number of days, the lender may begin foreclosure proceedings.
Demand	The payoff amount necessary to retire a secured debt.
Depreciation	A decline in the value of property. Usually due to the obsolescence or wear and tear of the improvements on the land or adverse changes in the neighborhood or real estate market.
Discharge	A document that ends a debtor's legally enforceable obligation to pay a debt.
Disclosure	Regarding real estate, it is revealing all known facts concerning the property being transferred.
Disposition Fee	"Workout fees" paid to a special servicer for making a loan current or liquidating a problem loan or foreclosed property. Can also include late fees, modification fees and loan administration charges.
Distressed Property	Property that is in poor physical or financial condition.
Down Payment	The upfront cash commitment paid by the buyer. It makes up the difference between the sales price of a property and the loan amount obtainable.
Due Diligence	A measure of prudence, activity, or assiduity, as is properly to be expected from, and ordinarily exercised by, a reasonable and prudent person under the particular circumstances; not measured by any absolute standard but depends on the relative facts of the special case.

"Due on Sale" Clause (DOS)	Provision in a mortgage or deed of trust calling for the total payoff of the loan balance in the event of a sale or transfer of title to the secured real property. A contract provision which authorizes the lender, at its option, to declare immediately due and payable sums secured by the lender's security instrument upon a sale of transfer of all or any part of the real property securing the loan without the lender's prior written consent. For purposes of this definition, a sale or transfer means the conveyance of real property of any right, title or interest therein, whether legal or equitable, whether voluntary or involuntary, by outright sale, deed, installment sale contract, land contract, contract for deed, leasehold interest with a term greater than three years, lease-option contract or any other method of conveyance of real property interests. Standard language which states that the loan must be paid when a house is sold.
Duress	Unlawful constraint or action exercised upon a person who is forced to perform an act against his or her will.
Earnest Money	An advance payment towards the purchase price of property that binds the parties to a purchase contract for property. It is usually not refundable if the purchase doesn't go through as a fault of the buyer, unless specified otherwise. Also known as Good Faith Deposit.
Emergency Petition	See "Bare Bones" petition.
Encumbrance	A legal right, claim or lien upon real property that diminishes the owner's equity or the land's value. Typical encumbrances are mortgages, trust deeds, judgments, assessments, mechanic's liens, easements, etc.
Equal Credit Opportunity Act	Prohibits discrimination in any aspect of a credit transaction on the basis of race, religion, age, color, national origin, receipt of public assistance funds, sex, or marital status.
Equity	The property's current value minus the sum of all liens against it.
Equity of Redemption	A right of the owner to reclaim property before it is sold through foreclosure by the payment of the debt, interest, and costs.

Escheat	The reversion of property to the state or county, as provided by state law, in cases where a decedent dies intestate without heirs capable of inheriting or when the property is abandoned.
Escrow	Amounts set aside for a particular purpose. For example, one type of escrow would be money paid to your mortgage company for payment of property taxes, and insurance.
Escrow Analysis	A lender's periodic examination of an escrow account to determine if the lender is withholding enough funds from a borrower's monthly mortgage payment to pay for expenses such as property taxes and insurance.
Estoppel	A bar to the assertion of a right or a defense in consequence of a previous position, act or representation.
Estoppel Certificate	A document in which a borrower certifies the amount he or she owes on a mortgage loan and rate of interest.
Exclusive Agency Listing	A listing contract under which the owner appoints a real estate broker as his or her exclusive agent for a designated period of time to sell the property, on the owner's stated terms, for a commission. The owner reserves the right to sell without paying anyone a commission.
Exclusive Right to Sell Listing	A listing contract under which the owner appoints a real estate broker as his or her exclusive agent for a designated period of time, to sell the property on the owner's stated terms, and agrees to pay the broker a commission when the property is sold whether by the broker, the owner, or another broker.
Eviction	A legal procedure to remove a tenant (including former homeowner) for reasons including failure to pay rent.
Exempt Property	Property that the law allows you to keep when you are faced with collection on an unsecured debt.
Exit Strategy	The way in which an investor closes out a specific investment, usually for cash.

Fair Debt Collection Practices Act	A federal law passed in 1977 which outlaws debtor harassment and other types of collection practices. The act regulates collection agencies, original creditors who set up a separate office to collect debts, and lawyers hired by the creditor to help collect overdue bills. An original creditor--the company or individual that originally granted the credit--is not covered by the act, but may be covered by similar measures approved by state governments.
Fair Market Value	The highest price a property in its as-is, where-is, with all faults condition, will bring on the open market, given an informed and freely willing buyer and seller.
Fannie Mae (FNMA)	Federal National Mortgage Association - the largest secondary-market investor in residential mortgages in the United States. Provides a constant and orderly market for banks to go to when they need to sell mortgages in order to keep their loan portfolios in balance with government-mandated liquidity ratios.
Freddie Mac (FHLMC)	**Federal Home Loan Mortgage Corporation** - a stockholder-owned corporation chartered by Congress to create a continuous flow of funds to mortgage lenders in support of homeownership and rental housing. Freddie Mac purchases single-family and multifamily residential mortgages from lenders and packages them into securities that are sold to investors.
FHA (FHA Loan)	Federal Housing Administration (formed in 1934). It's now a branch of HUD, whose basic function is to spur housing in the directions that Congress mandates by issuing mortgage insurance to institutional lenders on the loans they make under the 47 different loan programs that FHA now sponsors. With such loan insurance lenders are willing to lend with smaller down payments and at lower rates of interest. A loan insured by the Federal Housing Administration open to all qualified home purchasers. Interest rates on FHA loans are generally market rates, while down payment requirements are lower than for conventional loans. FHA loans cannot exceed the statutory limit.
Fiduciary	A person serving in a position of trust.
Fiduciary Duty	The relationship of trust that buyers and sellers expect from a real estate agent. The term also applies to legal and business relationships.

Flipping	Buying and then reselling property for a profit within a very short holding period.
Forbearance	A course of action a lender may pursue to delay foreclosure or legal action against a delinquent borrower.
Forbearance Agreement	A formal agreement between a borrower and a lender to temporarily postpone an ongoing foreclosure.
Foreclosure	The process by which a lender takes back a property on which the mortgagor has defaulted. A servicer may take over a property from a borrower on behalf of a lender. A property usually goes into the process of foreclosure if payments are more than 90 days past due.
For Sale By Owner (FSBO)	The owner markets and sells the home without using a licensed real estate broker to avoid paying a sales commission.
Fraud	Deception that causes a person to give up property, or a lawful right.
Fraudulent Transfer	Giving away property to keep it from creditors.
Free and Clear	Ownership of property free of all indebtedness. When an owner's equity is equal to the fair market value of her property.
Garnishment	A creditor's seizure, to satisfy a debt, of property belonging to the debtor that is in possession of a third party. An example would be the seizure of money from your bank account, or your wages (wage garnishment).
Good-Faith Estimate	An estimate from an institutional lender that shows the costs a borrower will incur, including loan-processing charges and inspection fees.
Grace Period	A period of days during which a debtor may cure a delinquency without penalty (before triggering a late charge, a foreclosure or an acceleration of the balance due).
Grantee	The person acquiring title to real property by a deed.
Grantor	The person transferring title to real property by a deed.
Hard Money Loan	A loan made based primarily upon the collateral's equity, rather than the creditworthiness of the Borrower.

Highest and Best Use	That possible use of land that would produce the greatest net income and thereby develop the highest land value.
Home Equity Line of Credit (HELOC)	A mortgage loan that works much like a charge card, wherein a homeowner borrows money as needed, up to a pre-negotiated limit. Interest is paid only on the amount of the loan used and the borrower can pay off the balance as quickly or as slowly as they like.
Home Equity Loan	Loan made to provide homeowners with access to excess built-up equity in their residence. Typically, secured by a junior lien mortgage where a superior lien mortgage exists.
Homesteading	A document that protects some of a home's equity from lawsuits.
HUD-1 Uniform Settlement Statement	A closing statement or settlement sheet that outlines all closing costs on a real estate transaction or refinancing.
Interest Rate Cap	Limits the interest rate or the interest rate adjustment to a specified maximum. This protects the borrower from increasing interest rates.
Institutional Lenders	Banks, Savings & Loan associations, and insurance companies who lend out depositors' money as contrasted with private individuals lending out personal funds.
Insolvent	A person or business that does not have sufficient assets to pay its debts.
Illiquid	Not readily convertible to cash.
Interest	The cost of using borrowed money. It's quoted as an annual percentage of the loan amount. The rate can either be fixed or fluctuate ("adjust") over the life of the loan.
Involuntary Lien	A lien imposed upon property by the operation of law rather than at the will of the owner. Property taxes, federal income taxes, bonded assessments and abstracts of judgment are examples of involuntary liens.
Involuntary Prepayment	Prepayment on a mortgage loan due to default

Joint Tenancy	An estate owned by two or more parties in equal shares that is created by a single transfer document. Upon the death of a joint tenant the surviving joint tenants take the entire decedent's share of the property, so nothing passes to the heirs of the deceased.
Judgment	The decision of a court or law. If a court decides that a person must repay a debt, a lien may be placed against that person's property.
Judgment Lien	A general lien (good for 10 years) created by a court ordering a debtor to pay a certain amount of money to the judgment creditor. The lien will bind to the debtor's real property once an abstract of the judgment is recorded. Thereafter the debtor won't be able to resell, refinance or buy any other property in the county without paying off the lien.
Judicial Foreclosure	A foreclosure that is processed via a court action. Usually limited to a collection action on an involuntary, judgment lien that automatically attached against a debtor's real property by operation of law (such as a recorded abstract of judgment).
Judgment Proof	People or businesses with property of minimal value, which can be entirely protected by exemptions, making it difficult or impossible for any creditor to force you to pay a debt.
Junior Bene Buyout	The purchase of a junior mortgagee or beneficiary's mortgage or trust deed position via an assignment at a steep discount because of an impending foreclosure on a senior mortgage or trust deed. If done correctly the new mortgagee/beneficiary will be paid in full via the resale or refinancing of the real property.
Junior Lien	A lien that does not have first claim on the property it is secured by because it was recorded later than a competing lien secured by the same property.
Junior Mortgage	A mortgage loan that is subordinate to the primary or senior loan(s).
Late Charge	A fee imposed on a borrower when the borrower does not make a payment on time.
Late Payment	A payment a lender receives after the due date has passed.

Lease Option	A lease that contains the right to purchase the property for a specific price within a certain time frame.
Leaseback	A transaction in which the buyer leases back the property to the seller for a specified period of time.
Leaseback with Exclusive Option to Repurchase	The Tenant enjoys an exclusive option to purchase the property at a predetermined price within the term of the Lease.
Lien	A claim against real property. Also called a 'security interest' or an 'attachment'.
Liquidation	The sale of a defaulted mortgage loan or of the REO property that previously secured the loan.
Lis Pendens	A recorded notice of pending litigation, the outcome of which could affect the title to a particular piece of property.
Listing Agreement	A limited-time agreement with a licensed real estate broker that authorizes the broker to represent the seller in the sale of their property.
Lock	A lender's promise to hold a certain interest rate and points for you, for a given number of days, while your loan application is processed.
Loan-To-Value (LTV)	The relationship between the dollar amount of the loan and the value of the property. For instance, a loan with a $70,000 loan balance on a property with a $100,000 value would result in an LTV of 70%. Lenders require a protective equity cushion between their loan positions and the fair market value of a secured property. Non-guaranteed lenders generally require that their loans amount to no more than 75% to 85% of their appraiser's estimate of the market value of the encumbered property.
Low-Ball Offer	An offer made to a seller that is substantially below their asking price, and/or market value.
Marketable Title	A title that is free and clear of objectionable liens, clouds, or other title defects. A title which enables an owner to sell his property freely to others and which others will accept without objection.

Market Conditions	Factors affecting the sale and purchase of homes at a particular point in time.
Market Value	The highest price which a buyer, willing, but not compelled, would pay, and the lowest price a seller, willing but not compelled to sell, would accept. The current value of property as determined by exposure to offers from willing buyers in the open market.
Mechanic's Lien	A non-voluntary, statutory lien recorded against a specific property in favor of contractors/materialmen for unpaid improvements made to the property. A mechanic's lien priority is established when the improvements were begun (visible to the eye test) rather than when it was recorded. The lien must be coupled with a court action to be perfected
Memorandum of Agreement	Writing meant to memorialize the essentials of a transaction or act as an actual contract.
Modification	A change in any of the terms of the loan agreement.
Mortgage	A written pledge of property that is put up as security for the repayment of a loan. The lender is the mortgagee and the property owner is the mortgagor.
Mortgage Banker	A loan originator that uses its own funds to make real estate loans which it then resells to long term mortgage investors.
Mortgage Broker	An agent that matches borrowers with lenders in exchange for a referral fee that amounts to part or all of the "loan points" being charged the borrower.
Mortgage Insurance Premium	The payment made by a borrower to the lender for transmittal to HUD to help defray the cost of the FHA mortgage insurance program and to provide a reserve fund to protect lenders against loss in insured mortgage transactions. In FHA insured mortgages this represents an annual rate of one-half of one percent paid by the mortgagor on a monthly basis.
Mortgage Servicer	A bank, mortgage company, or similar business that communicates with property owners concerning their mortgage loans. The servicer usually works for another company that owns the mortgage. A mortgage servicer may accept and record payments, negotiate workouts, and supervise the foreclosure process in the event of a default.

Motivated Seller	Any seller with a strong incentive to make a deal.
Multifamily Property	A building with five or more residential units, usually classified as a high rise, low rise or a garden apartment.
Multiple Listing Service (MLS)	The combined property listings of local real estate brokers, /members that are pooled together in an MLS book and computer network for the widest marketing exposure to their membership at large.
Negative Amortization	Occurs when interest accrued during a payment period is greater than the scheduled payment and the excess amount is added to the outstanding loan balance. For example, if the interest rate on an ARM exceeds the interest rate cap, then the borrower's payment will not be sufficient to cover the interest accrued during the billing period. The unpaid interest is added to the outstanding loan balance.
Net Operating Income (NOI)	Total income less operating expenses, adjustments, etc., but before mortgage payments, tenant improvements and leasing commissions.
Non-Assumption Clause	A loan provision that prohibits the transfer of a mortgage to another borrower without lender approval.
Non-Judicial Foreclosure	Non-judicial foreclosures are processed without court intervention, with the requirements for the foreclosure established by state statutes.
Nonconforming Loan	Loans that do not comply with FNMA or Freddie Mac guidelines. These guidelines establish the maximum loan amount, down payment, borrower credit and income requirements, and suitable properties. Loans that do conform to these guidelines may be sold to Fannie Mae or Freddie Mac.
Notary Public	A bonded officer licensed by the state to "acknowledge and attest" to the validity of signatures of others. Notarized signatures are required of the general public for any documents that individuals record in order to prevent the perpetration of fraud by forgery.

Notice of Default (NOD)	To initiate a non-judicial foreclosure proceeding involving a public sale of the real property securing the deed of trust, the trustee under the deed of trust records a Notice of Default and Election to Sell ("NOD") the real property collateral in the public records.
Offer and Acceptance	Two essential components of a valid contract; when all parties agree to the exact terms.
Option	A legal right to purchase property at some future date for a specified price and terms. The right is forfeited if not exercised in time.
Oral	By mouth; not written; verbal; spoken.
Overbid	That amount of money bid in excess of the trustee's or sheriff's minimum bid. It is distributed, pro tanto, to the succeeding equity holders.
Partial Claim	A loss mitigation technique used with HUD insured loans wherein HUD pays a claim to the loan servicer which brings the account current.
Per-Diem Interest	Interest charged or accrued daily.
Personal Property	Property that is movable or harvestable, i.e. securities, furniture, cars, promissory notes, clothing, intangibles, etc.
Physical Deterioration	Loss of value due to wear and tear or action of the elements.
P.I.T.I.	Refers to the monthly housing expenses of: Principal, Interest, Taxes and Insurance
Plaintiff	The person or business that initiates a lawsuit.
Points	A charge made by a lender that's part of the borrower's cost of obtaining a loan. Each point equals one percent (1%) of the loan amount. Points increase the effective yield on the loan above the nominal interest rate being charged.
Posting	Giving notice by physically attaching it to a prescribed bulletin board and/or attaching it to the affected property itself.
Postponement	An oral announcement, made in lieu of a scheduled sheriff's or trustee's sale, which reschedules the pending sale.

Power of Attorney	A document that authorizes an individual to act on behalf of someone else.
Pre-Approval Letter	A letter from a lender that informs a seller about the amount of money that a potential buyer can obtain.
Preliminary Title Report	A title company report showing the open title record of a property prior to the issuance of a title insurance policy.
Prepayment Penalty	A fee charged by a lender if a loan is paid off earlier than required.
Present Owner Judgment Search	A credit/lien search for municipal liens, a search for civil judgments, bankruptcy, and other docketed matters resulting in a lien on real property.
Prepayment Premium	A penalty paid by the borrower for any prepayments made on a mortgage loan if required under the loan documents. The premium is usually set at a fixed rate which, at times, decreases in steps as the loan matures.
Prepayment Risk	The risk that a borrower will repay the remaining principal or an amount other than the scheduled payment on a mortgage prior to maturity, thus shortening the life of the loan. In order to reduce prepayment risk, commercial mortgages commonly have lockout periods and/or prepayment premiums or yield maintenance.
Presale	Sale of property in anticipation of foreclosure or repossession, usually with the lender's consent.
Principal	The amount of money owed on a loan, excluding interest and other charges.
Priority	The superiority of an interest relative to other interests on the same property. Generally, the first to record is first in right.
Priority Clause	A clause in a subordinate lien (such as a 2nd trust deed) which states that it is subject to a prior lien.
Private Mortgage Insurance (PMI)	Insurance against a loss by a lender, due to a default in payments from a borrower. Often required when a buyer is paying a small down payment (less than 20% of the appraised value of the secured property)

Probate	The process by which a court changes the title to a deceased person's real property. The property is from a decedent to either: 1) his or her heirs (as determined under the laws of intestacy), called an "intestate estate"; or 2) pursuant to the terms of his or her will or trust, called a "testate estate". All techniques which "avoid probate" involve changing title to the decedent's real property without court involvement.
Promissory Note	An unconditional instrument of indebtedness between borrower and lender (containing all of the terms of the loan) that is commonly secured by a mortgage (mortgage note) or deed of trust.
Puffing	Exaggerated or superlative comments or opinions not made as representations of fact and thus not grounds for misrepresentation.
Qualifying Ratios	Lenders compute qualifying ratios to determine how much a potential buyer can borrow.
Reaffirmation	An agreement in the bankruptcy process to pay back a debt that would otherwise be discharged in bankruptcy.
Real Estate Broker	Any person, partnership, association, or corporation who sells (or offers to sell), buys (or offers to buy) or negotiates the purchase, sale, or exchange of real estate, or who leases (or offers to lease) or rents (or offers to rent) any real estate or the improvements thereon for others and for a compensation or valuable consideration.
Real Estate Owned (REO)	The term used to describe real property collateral to which title has been taken back by the mortgagee (trust by way of beneficial ownership) through foreclosure or deed in lieu of foreclosure.
Real Estate Settlement Procedures Act (RESPA)	A federal law designed to make sellers and buyers aware of settlement fees and other transaction-related costs.
Realized Loss	The amount of principals, interest and fees that is not realized (unrecovered) from the sale of a defaulted mortgage loan or sale of foreclosed REO property. It is equal to the amount of (a) the outstanding principal balance of the loan plus (b) all unpaid scheduled interest plus (c) all fees applied to the sale of the property minus (d) the amount received from liquidation.

Realtor ™	A designation for a broker, or broker's agent who is a member of the National Association of Realtors, a trade group.
Recording	Filing a document with the county recorder to have it entered into the public record, giving constructive notice to the public at large of its contents. Establishes priority amongst competing claims.
Redeem	Recovering collateral from a creditor by paying the entire amount you owe. In bankruptcy, property can be redeemed in some situations by paying the collateral's value even if that amount is less than the entire amount owed.
Redemption Period	A period of time established by state law during which a property owner has the right to redeem his or her property from a forced, public foreclosure sale.
Redemptive Right	Generally refers to a debtor's right to reacquire title to property lost via a judicial foreclosure (germane to mortgage states) within a year or so afterward. It also refers to IRS's right to redeem property that had secured a federal tax lien prior to a non-judicial foreclosure by a senior lien. IRS's right is limited to 120 days after the sheriff's sale or trustee's sale and requires reimbursement to the winning bidder of the trustee's sale.
Refinancing	The process of paying back old debts by borrowing new money.
Regulation Z	The federal code issued under the Truth-in-Lending Act which requires that a borrower be advised in writing of all costs associated with the credit portion of a financial transaction.
Reinstatement	The process of remedying a default so that a lender will view your loan as current.
Relief from Automatic Stay	An order from the bankruptcy court allowing a lender to proceed with the default remedies (e.g. sheriff's sale or trustee's sale) against a debtor - exempt from the automatic, protective shield of the bankruptcy court.
Repayment Plan	When a borrower falls behind in mortgage payments, many lenders will negotiate a repayment plan rather than go to initiate foreclosure proceedings.
Repossession	When a house is repossessed, it is taken back by the lender holding the mortgage.

Rescission	The right of cancellation of a contract, generally within three business days of a transaction. This is called the "right of rescission," and it is guaranteed by the Federal Truth in Lending Act.
Right of Redemption	In certain states, the Trustor under the deed of trust, or mortgagor under the mortgage, and/or junior lien holders have the right to redeem the real property following foreclosure sale. The period of time during which the property may be redeemed, if right of redemption is permitted and whether it is applicable to non-judicial and/or judicial foreclosure, varies significantly by state and can be as little as three months or more than a year.
Sales Comparison Approach	The process of estimating the value of a property by examining and comparing actual sales of comparable properties.
Seasoning	The length of time since origination of a mortgage loan. The longer a loan has been outstanding and performing to its terms, the better "seasoned" it is. A loan that has been outstanding, for say three years, but shows a poor pay history, i.e., several late pays, particularly beyond 30 days, is not considered seasoned because of its performance.
Secondary Market	Most lenders sell the loans they originate to large-scale, national investors such as "Fannie Mae" and Freddie Mac". The reason they do is to recycle their money to create more loans (on which they collect loan origination fees, points, etc.). In order to sell their loans originating lenders have to adhere to Fannie Mae's underwriting guidelines.
Second Mortgage	A mortgage in addition to the first mortgage. Home equity loans, credit lines, home improvement loans are second mortgage loans. Second mortgage is subordinate to the first one. Second mortgage loans are nonconforming loans, so, they usually carry a higher interest rate, and they often are for a shorter time.
Section 8	A federal, rental (and purchase) assistance program under HUD for very-low-income families. The money is funneled to local housing authorities who pay (directly to landlords) the difference between market rent and what eligible families can afford to pay. The housing "voucher" program is a more flexible variant where the recipient families freely rent whatever they want for whatever rental amount they choose to pay.

Self-Amortizing Loans	Loans for which the full amount of the principal sum borrower will be completely paid off at the loan's termination pursuant to the loan's payment schedule.
Settlement Statement	A document that details who has paid what to whom.
Sheriff's Deed	The deed issued by a sheriff to the highest bidder at a sheriff's sale.
Sheriff's Sale	The sale of property by the sheriff under authority of a court's judgment and writ of execution in order to satisfy an unpaid judgment, mortgage, lien, or other debt of the owner.
Short Sale	A type of preforeclosure sale in which the mortgagee agrees to let you sell the property for less than the full amount due, and accept the proceeds as payment in full. The sale of property at a fair market price that's lower than the loan balance(s).
Soldier's and Sailor's Relief Act	Protects certain military personnel from losing their homes to foreclosure while on they're on active duty.
Specific Performance Suit	A legal action brought in court of equity in special cases to compel a party to carry out the terms of a contract.
Subject To	The purchase of a property with an existing lien against the title without assuming any personal liability for its payment.
Sub-Performing Loan	A loan that is making payments but not the full principal and interest payments that the Mortgage Note demands. Many investors also classify a loan as sub-performing even if monthly payments are current but when the loan to value ratio or other primary value indicator is such that it is unlikely that the loan will be unable to pay off in full at maturity.
Suit to Quiet Title	A court action intended to establish or settle the title to a particular property, especially when there is a cloud on the title.
Summons	This is a document at the beginning of a lawsuit to tell the defendant what is being requested, and what must be done to respond to the complaint.
Tax Deed	An instrument, similar to certificate of sale, given to a purchaser at a tax sale.

Tax Lien	An encumbrance placed upon a property as a claim for payment of a tax liability. A tax lien may be imposed for failure to pay city, county, estate, income, payroll, property, sales, or school taxes. Tax liens and assessments take priority over most, if not all other liens.
Tax Sale	The public sale of a property by the government for nonpayment of taxes.
"Time is of the Essence"	A phrase in a contract that requires the performance of a certain act within a stated period of time.
Title	Evidence that the owner of land is in lawful possession thereof, evidence of ownership.
Title Search	A detailed check of the title records at the recorder's office to make certain that the buyer is purchasing a property from the legal owner and that there are no more liens against the property's title than those already disclosed by the seller.
Transfer Tax	A tax collected from sellers upon the transfer of their title to real property (see Closing Costs).
Trust	A legal arrangement where a person, called the grantor or testator, transfers assets to a person called a Trustee who will manage those assets for the benefit of the beneficiary.
Trust Deed	An instrument used to create a mortgage lien by which the mortgagor conveys his or her title to a trustee, who holds it as security for the benefit of the note holder (the lender) also called a deed of trust.
Trustee	The Trustee represents the Trust that holds the legal title to the collateral for the benefit of all class holders of the security. It must carry out its duties according to the indentures established within the Trust Indenture.
Trustee's Deed	The deed issued by a trustee to the highest bidder at a trustee's sale. The deed discloses on its face what the opening or minimum bid was at the sale and what the final winning bid actually amounted to.
Trustee's Responsibilities	In general, the duties of a trustee are to honestly represent the best interests of the beneficiary. The trust agreement itself may set forth other more specific duties.

Trustee's Sale	A non-judicial auction sale of real property, conducted by a trustee in the exercise of the power of sale clause, pursuant to the terms of the defaulted deed of trust.
Truth In Lending Act	Under this act a lender is required to provide you with a disclosure estimating the costs of the loan you have applied for, including your total finance charge and the Annual Percentage Rate (APR) within three business days of your application for a loan.
Unrecorded Deed	An unrecorded deed transfers ownership from one party to another without being officially recorded.
Unsecured Debt	A debt that is not secured by any pledge of property. Examples: utility bills, student loans, credit cards, medical, hospital, or doctors' bills, etc.
Usury	A rate of interest charged on a loan that is in excess of the statutory maximum.
Veterans Administration (VA)	Established under the Servicemen's Readjustment Act of 1944. It provides two very helpful housing benefits to servicemen and veterans by guaranteeing a lender's housing loan made to an eligible vet without any down payment requirement and by requiring that the subject property conform to VA's housing standards as determined by an on-site appraisal conducted by an approved VA appraiser.
Valid Contract	A contract that complies with all the essentials of a contract and is binding and enforceable on all parties to it.
Variable Rate Loan	A loan bearing an interest rate that fluctuates (vs. a fixed rate) according to some specified financial index of the current cost of money - wherein both the interest rate and the monthly payment are subject to adjustment at some pre-established interval.
Voidable Contract	A contract that seems to be valid on the surface, but may be rejected or disaffirmed by one of the parties.
Void Contract	A contract that has no legal force or effect because it does not meet the essential elements of a contract.
Voluntary Lien	Any lien placed on property with the consent and cooperation of the owner (mortgage).

Warranty Deed

A deed containing express and implied covenants as to good title and right to possession.

Workout

A workout can be a variety of negotiated agreements you might arrange with creditors to address a debt that you are having trouble paying. Most commonly, a workout is devised between a mortgagee, and mortgagor to restructure or modify a loan to avoid foreclosure.

Wraparound Mortgage

A loan arrangement whereby the existing loan is retained and a new loan is added to the property. Full payments on both mortgages are made to the wraparound mortgagee, who then forwards the payments on the first mortgage to the first mortgagee.

Additional Notes

_____

_____

_____

_____

_____

_____

_____

_____

_____

_____

_____

_____

_____

_____

_____

_____

_____

_____

_____

_____

_____

_____

Additional Notes

Additional Notes

_____

_____

_____

_____

_____

_____

_____

_____

_____

_____

_____

_____

_____

_____

_____

_____

_____

_____

_____

_____

_____

_____

_____

About Dominion Foreclosure Consulting Services, Inc.

Dominion's primary focus is offering Foreclosure Consulting services to the general public. The onset of new foreclosure real estate laws have allowed us to focus strictly on ensuring that the property owner's rights are clearly explained, that all avenues of rectification are fully exhausted, and that a financially satisfactory solution is reached.

For more information on services, seminars, and speaking engagements, please visit our website at **www.dfcscorp.com**!

Dominion Foreclosure Consulting Services, Inc.
P.O. Box 121
Thomasville, North Carolina 27361-0121

info@foreclosureworkbook.com
www.foreclosureworkbook.com
www.dfcscorp.com

ATTENTION!
We would love to hear your comments and testimonials!

Your comments make a big difference in the development and revision of our books and services. Please take a few moments to register your comments with us. Not only will your input make a difference, you'll receive special offers available only to registered owners of our books on specialized products and services.

REGISTER NOW BY:

PHONE	FAX	EMAIL	or MAIL us
877-834-5930	877-834-5930	info@foreclosureworkbook.com	this registration card!

fold here

- -

REGISTRATION CARD
NAME   DATE
ADDRESS
CITY   STATE   ZIP
PHONE   EMAIL
WHERE DID YOU HEAR ABOUT THIS PRODUCT?
WHERE DID YOU PURCHASE THIS PRODUCT?
DID YOU FIND THIS BOOK HELPFUL? (VERY) 5 4 3 2 1 (NOT AT ALL)
COMMENTS
WAS IT EASY TO USE? (VERY EASY) 5 4 3 2 1 (NOT AT ALL)
We occasionally make our mailing list available to carefully selected companies whose products may be of interest to you.
☐   If you do not wish to receive mailings from these companies, please check this box.
☐   You can quote me in future DFCS, Inc. promotional materials.

Dominion Foreclosure Consulting Services, Inc.
P.O. Box 121
Thomasville, NC 27361-0121
Attn: Testimonials

Printed in the United States
119024LV00001BB/62/A

9 781602 669680